# NEW DIRECTIONS FOR YOUTH DEVELOPMENT

*Theory*
*Practice*
*Research*

summer | 2007

# Summertime

## Confronting Risks, Exploring Solutions

# WITHDRAWN

## UTSA LIBRARIES

**Ron Fairchild**
**Gil G. Noam**

*issue*
*editors*

JOSSEY-BASS™
An Imprint of
WILEY

Summertime: Confronting Risks, Exploring Solutions
*Ron Fairchild, Gil G. Noam* (eds.)
New Directions for Youth Development, No. 114, Summer 2007
*Gil G. Noam*, Editor-in-Chief

Microfilm copies of issues and articles are available in 16mm and 35mm, as well as microfiche in 105mm, through University Microfilms Inc., 300 North Zeeb Road, Ann Arbor, Michigan 48106-1346.

NEW DIRECTIONS FOR YOUTH DEVELOPMENT (ISSN 1533-8916, electronic ISSN 1537-5781) is part of The Jossey-Bass Psychology Series and is published quarterly by Wiley Subscription Services, Inc., A Wiley Company, at Jossey-Bass, 989 Market Street, San Francisco, California 94103-1741. POSTMASTER: Send address changes to New Directions for Youth Development, Jossey-Bass, 989 Market Street, San Francisco, California 94103-1741.

SUBSCRIPTIONS cost $80.00 for individuals and $195.00 for institutions, agencies, and libraries. Prices subject to change. Refer to the order form at the back of this issue.

EDITORIAL CORRESPONDENCE should be sent to the Editor-in-Chief, Dr. Gil G. Noam, McLean Hospital, 115 Mill Street, Belmont, MA 02478.

Cover photograph by Will Kirk

www.josseybass.com

Wiley Bicentennial Logo: Richard J. Pacifico

# Contents

# Editors' Notes

HOW DID YOU SPEND your summer break when you were a child? Most Americans have an idyllic image of summer as a carefree, happy time when "kids can be kids" and enjoy experiences like taking vacations, relaxing at the pool, and spending time with family. Yet, the reality of what many children encounter during the summer months is anything but idyllic and carefree.

Whereas wealthier children and youth typically access a wide variety of resources that help them grow both academically and developmentally over the summer, poorer children often are unable to benefit from similar types of experiences. When the school doors close, many youth across the country exit into an environment lacking educational opportunities, healthy meals, and adequate supervision from caring adults. From a resources perspective, summer break in the United States has traditionally been a time when the rich get richer and the poor get poorer.

This volume of *New Directions for Youth Development* focuses critical attention on the resource disparity created by the traditional summer break for U.S. schoolchildren. The chapters that follow bring together scholars and practitioners with unique perspectives on the need for summer learning opportunities for children living in poverty and how best to accomplish that goal. By exploring recent developments in the field of summer learning, hopefully the chapters that follow will help foster dialogue and contribute to enduring solutions to one of the most persistent barriers to educational equity in America.

When read together, these chapters constitute a compelling case for large-scale public investments in high-quality summer learning

NEW DIRECTIONS FOR YOUTH DEVELOPMENT, NO. 114, SUMMER 2007 © WILEY PERIODICALS, INC.
Published online in Wiley InterScience (www.interscience.wiley.com) • DOI: 10.1002/yd.208

opportunities for youth from lower-income households as a strategy for narrowing the achievement gap. The first two chapters of this volume document groundbreaking evidence about the academic and nutritional setbacks that young people face during the summer months. Karl L. Alexander and his colleagues have spent nearly three decades investigating the learning patterns and life trajectories of the same group of young people from Baltimore in their Beginning School Study. One of the most striking findings from their work is that early differences in summer learning opportunities have lasting repercussions throughout a young person's educational development, accounting in part for later educational outcomes such as high school completion and college enrollment. This analysis adds to a well-established research base of at least thirty-nine empirical studies over the past hundred years that confirm a pattern of summer learning loss, particularly for low-income students. Chapter One also provides a research-based rationale for policymakers and providers who place a high priority on preventative summer learning programs at younger grade levels.

In Chapter Two, Douglas B. Downey and Heather R. Boughton expand the evidence of summer loss beyond academic regression in reading or mathematical skills. Their research examines the powerful role that nutritional setbacks over the summer months play in contributing to the epidemic of childhood obesity in America. Although the federally subsidized meal program is available to millions of children from September to June, only one in five students who participate during the school year has access to those meals during the summer. The alarming pattern of changes in body mass index rates over the summer months underscores the need to extend nutrition programs to more young people during the summer months.

The remaining chapters in this volume focus on solutions and strategies for addressing the lack of resources available for youth from lower-income households during the summer months. In Chapter Three, Susanne R. Bell and Natalie Carrillo describe the characteristics of highly effective summer learning programs and provide an overview of some of the most successful model programs from around the country. The authors of Chapters Four,

Five, and Six focus on some of the unique aspects of programs that serve youth in rural areas, employ partnerships to create effective programming, and develop young people's reading abilities. Although there are important differences among the programs, there is also a growing consensus on the core elements of high-quality summer learning programs. The authors define *quality* programming during the summer months and present a clear vision of how to make the promise of an enriching and productive summer break a reality for more young people.

The final two chapters of this issue focus on two of the most salient and timely issues currently facing the field: program evaluation and sustainability. In Chapter Seven, Earl Martin Phalen and Tiffany M. Cooper describe the process Building Educated Leaders for Life (BELL) uses to engage in ongoing rigorous evaluation to drive program improvement. Rather than framing the need to measure results and impact as something imposed on programs by external forces (that is, funders and government agencies), the authors show the power of internally motivated evaluations focused on achieving higher levels of program quality and growth.

In the final chapter, M. Jane Sundius offers an insightful perspective from the funding community about the challenge of generating large-scale, sustainable public investment in summer learning programs. Whereas private foundation support continues to be an important source of revenue for many programs, favorable public policies and investments offer the best hope of equitable access to high-quality programs at a large scale in the future. Chapter Eight offers an agenda for decision makers who seek to build coordinated systems and policies that support summer learning opportunities. Despite the unequivocal need for summer programs, particularly for disadvantaged children and youth, surprisingly few policies specifically target summer as a time to advance learning, support healthy physical and emotional development, and provide safe, engaging environments for young people while the school doors are closed. At this point, public policy has yet to be developed and is lagging behind the growing field of summer programming.

This journal was designed to both highlight and stimulate growth in the field of summer learning. As editors of this volume, our intention is to attract attention to summer as a critical window of time for young people's academic, social, emotional, and physical development. We also seek to strengthen the position of the summer learning field within the broader context of out-of-school-time programming. We encourage you to think critically about how your work intersects with the needs of young people over the summer months and how together we can achieve the goal of a more sustainable and equitable expansion of summer learning opportunities for all young people.

Ron Fairchild
Gil G. Noam
*Editors*

RON FAIRCHILD *is the executive director of the Center for Summer Learning at the Johns Hopkins University School of Education. The center works to create high-quality summer learning opportunities for all young people.*

GIL G. NOAM *is a clinical and developmental psychologist on the faculty of Harvard University and the founder and director of the Program in Education, Afterschool and Resiliency at Harvard Medical School and McLean Hospital.*

# Executive Summary

## Chapter One: Summer learning and its implications: Insights from the Beginning School Study

Karl L. Alexander, Doris R. Entwisle, Linda Steffel Olson

There is perhaps no more pressing issue in school policy today than the achievement gap across social lines. Achievement differences between well-to-do children and poor children and between disadvantaged racial and ethnic minorities and majority whites are large when children first begin school, and they increase over time. Despite years of study and an abundance of good intentions, these patterned achievement differences persist, but who is responsible, and how are schools implicated? The increasing gap seems to suggest that schools are unable to equalize educational opportunity or, worse still, that they actively handicap disadvantaged children. But a seasonal perspective on learning yields a rather different impression. Comparing achievement gains separately over the school year and the summer months reveals that much of the achievement gap originates over the summer period, when children are not in school. The authors review Beginning School Study research on differential summer learning across social lines (that is, by family socioeconomic level) and its implications for later schooling outcomes, including high school curriculum placements, high school dropout, and college attendance. These studies document the extent to which these large summer learning differences impede the later educational progress of children of low socioeconomic status. Practical

implications are discussed, including the need for early and sustained interventions to prevent the achievement gap from opening wide in the first place and for high-quality summer programming focused on preventing differential summer learning loss.

## Chapter Two: Childhood body mass index gain during the summer versus during the school year

**Douglas B. Downey, Heather R. Boughton**

The nationwide increase in obesity affects all population sectors, but the impact on children is of special concern because overweight children are prone to becoming overweight adults. Contrary to the opinion of experts, research suggests that schools may be more part of the solution than the problem. Recent seasonal comparison research (comparing children's outcomes during the summer and during school year) reports that children gain body mass index (BMI) nearly twice as fast during the summer as during the school year. Whereas most children experience healthier BMI gain during the school year than the summer, this is especially the case for black and Hispanic children and for children already overweight.

## Chapter Three: Characteristics of effective summer learning programs in practice

**Susanne R. Bell, Natalie Carrillo**

The Center for Summer Learning examined various summer program models and found that there are nine characteristics that provide a framework for effective summer programs. In this chapter, the authors demonstrate how effective practices lead to positive results for young people.

The nine characteristics of effective summer learning programs are (1) accelerating learning, (2) youth development, (3) proactive approach to summer learning, (4) leadership, (5) advanced planning,

NEW DIRECTIONS FOR YOUTH DEVELOPMENT • DOI: 10.1002/yd

(6) staff development, (7) strategic partnerships, (8) evaluation and commitment to program improvement, and (9) sustainability and cost-effectiveness. These characteristics are divided into two sections. The first three characteristics address a program's approach to learning. Summer instructional techniques are most effective when academic learning is woven into enrichment activities and youth development. The second section covers program infrastructure to ensure the organization achieves and maintains quality programming. The nine characteristics complement each other to ensure a strong program that works to prevent summer learning loss and narrow the achievement gap.

To demonstrate the variety of high-quality programs that include the nine characteristics, thirteen program profiles at the conclusion of the chapter each highlight one of the characteristics. These profiles show the various approaches that different summer programs have developed to accelerate academic achievement and promote positive development for young people in their communities.

## Chapter Four: Summer programming in rural communities: Unique challenges

**Ruthellen Phillips, Stacey Harper, Susan Gamble**

During the past several decades, child poverty rates have been higher in rural than in urban areas, and now 2.5 million children live in deep poverty in rural America. Studies indicate that poor children are most affected by the typical "summer slide." Summer programming has the ability to address the issues of academic loss, nutritional loss, and the lack of safe and constructive enrichment activities. However, poor rural communities face three major challenges in implementing summer programming: community resources, human capital, and accessibility. The success of Energy Express, a statewide award-winning six-week summer reading and nutrition program in West Virginia, documents strategies for overcoming the challenges faced by poor, rural communities in providing summer programs.

Energy Express (1) uses community collaboration to augment resources and develop community ownership, (2) builds human capital and reverses the acknowledged brain drain by engaging college students and community volunteers in meaningful service, and (3) increases accessibility through creative transportation strategies. West Virginia University Extension Service, the outreach arm of the land-grant institution, partners with AmeriCorps, a national service program, and various state and local agencies and organizations to implement a program that produces robust results.

## Chapter Five: Collaboration: Leveraging resources and expertise

**Anne Byrne, Jane Hansberry**

Successful collaboration is an art form but can be developed through several smart practices. The authors discuss the meaning of collaboration, stakeholder perceptions of collaborative partnerships, and the experience of Summer Scholars, a nonprofit community organization that successfully uses collaboration to accomplish its mission. Further, they offer strategies for successful collaborative efforts.

## Chapter Six: Summer library reading programs

**Carole D. Fiore**

Virtually all public libraries in the United States provide some type of summer library reading program during the traditional summer vacation period. Summer library reading programs provide opportunities for students of many ages and abilities to practice their reading skills and maintain skills that are developed during the school year. Fiore summarizes some of the research in the field and relates it to library programs and usage by students. Several traditional and innovative programs from U.S. and Canadian libraries are described. She concludes with a call for further research related to summer library reading programs.

## Chapter Seven: Using evaluation to improve program quality based on the BELL model

### Earl Martin Phalen, Tiffany M. Cooper

Building Educated Leaders for Life (BELL) is a national not-for-profit organization whose mission is to increase the educational achievements, self-esteem, and life opportunities of elementary school children living in low-income urban communities. BELL has been engaged in formal evaluation, internally and externally, for more than five years and has built internal evaluation capacity by investing in a specialized full-time evaluation team. As part of a continuous program improvement model of evaluation, BELL uses the data to refine program implementation and replicate successful elements of the services and operations. In this chapter, the authors highlight best practices from the field by outlining BELL's approach to using evaluation data for continuous program improvement. Key strategies include (1) carefully identifying intended users of the evaluation throughout the organization and among its external stakeholders, then working closely with intended users throughout the evaluation process, ensuring full engagement at every step of the process; (2) reporting findings in a readable, user-friendly format and timing the reporting so that it is aligned with programmatic decision making and planning cycles; and (3) making and supporting explicit recommendations for the next program cycle, where intended users have agreed to recommendations and ownership is assigned. BELL's successful use of data for improvement is evidenced by the consistently strong outcomes for the students it serves as well as increased efficiency and satisfaction related to service delivery that has supported the replication of BELL's programs nationally.

NEW DIRECTIONS FOR YOUTH DEVELOPMENT • DOI: 10.1002/yd

## *Chapter Eight: Finding the resources for summer learning programs*

**M. Jane Sundius**

Research on summer learning losses has unambiguous implications for America: all children need learning opportunities in the summer. But how and when policymakers, educators, and youth service providers will fashion appropriate programming are far less clear. At the root of this problem is the need to vastly increase, stabilize, and coordinate resources for summer programming. Jane Sundius first outlines the current landscape of summer programs. She then goes on to make the case that two key strategies are necessary to securing sustainable increases in funding that will allow all children access to summer programming. The first is a national advocacy and public will-building campaign. The second is extensive, local, public-private planning to map existing summer resources and needs and to create blueprints for programming that serve all children in communities. Drawing on her experiences as a foundation program director, Sundius urges programs, foundation officials, and other stakeholders to expand their summer funding efforts beyond individual summer programs and to support, in addition, strategic communications and community planning efforts that are aimed at providing summer learning opportunities for all children.

*A large portion of the achievement gap originates over the summer, when children are not in school. The resource disparity children from lower-income families experience fuels this achievement gap growth.*

# 1

# Summer learning and its implications: Insights from the Beginning School Study

*Karl L. Alexander, Doris R. Entwisle,*
*Linda Steffel Olson*

THE SCHOOL-YEAR CALENDAR in the United States, a relic from the country's early agrarian and urban history,[1] is a good bit shorter than that of most other industrial and industrializing countries. In 1990, the standard U.S. school year was 180 days.[2] That places us just ahead of Belgium and tied with Quebec, Spain, and Sweden toward the bottom of a list of twenty-five countries and far behind the leaders: Japan, 243 days; West Germany, between 244 and 266 days; South Korea, 220; and Israel and Luxembourg, 216. And despite a deep commitment to local governance in other areas of education policy and practice, the U.S. school calendar approaches a national template. In 2000, thirty of the forty-four states with statewide policies had school years of exactly 180 days.[3] A mere three required more than 180 days (Kansas tops the list at 186 days), while eleven required fewer (the lowest being North Dakota's 173 days).

NEW DIRECTIONS FOR YOUTH DEVELOPMENT, NO. 114, SUMMER 2007 © WILEY PERIODICALS, INC.
Published online in Wiley InterScience (www.interscience.wiley.com) • DOI: 10.1002/yd.210

11

The situation in Maryland, where our research is conducted, is fairly typical. In 2003–04, the school year was lengthened from 180 to 185 days, but typically a few days are missed each year owing to inclement weather, and the mandated minimum number of required days remains 180. For the 2004–05 school year, classes began on September 7; the previous year, they ended June 24. That interval of eleven weeks, or just under three months, is ample time for children to forget some of what they had learned the previous year and slip into bad habits.

Of course, not all school districts follow exactly the same schedule, and many localities have been experimenting with alternative school-year calendars, adding extra days or, more often, scheduling shorter breaks throughout the year, so-called balanced, modified, or year-round calendars.[4] Summer schools likewise have proliferated, sometimes for enrichment but more often for remediation as an alternative to grade retention. A survey of the nation's one hundred largest school systems reported some kind of summer programming in all one hundred, including a remedial component in ninety-two of the one hundred.[5] Twenty-five years earlier, probably just half of these school systems had summer programs.[6]

Despite these developments, most students in the United States still do not attend school during the summer, and calendar experimentation remains the exception. During the 2002–03 school year, an estimated 2.3 million children in K–12 attended public schools with modified school-year calendars,[7] less than 5 percent of that year's roughly 48 million public school enrollment. And in 1996, the most recent year for which we could find comprehensive data, just 9.2 percent of the K–12 enrollment attended summer programs,[8] with enrollments higher at the upper grades than at the elementary level.[9]

So despite the recent uptick in summer programming and scheduling reforms, most U.S. children still experience a long layoff from school during the summer months. How this affects their learning has commanded considerable attention. Interest in the topic dates back to the early part of the twentieth century,[10] but it was Barbara Heyns's comparison of school-year and summer achievement gains for a sample of Atlanta, Georgia, middle schoolers, published in

NEW DIRECTIONS FOR YOUTH DEVELOPMENT • DOI: 10.1002/yd

1978 as *Summer Learning and the Effects of Schooling*,[11] that first connected summer learning loss to the achievement gap issue.

Heyns's great insight was that the school-year calendar affords leverage for understanding achievement differences across social lines, by race or ethnicity and family income, for example. There is much concern in the current No Child Left Behind era about the achievement gap across social lines, and for good reason. We know that the achievement levels of poor and disadvantaged minority youth typically lag behind those of better-off children in the early grades and that over time they fall even farther back.[12] This achievement shortfall has important consequences: low test scores in the upper grades, for example, are associated with high levels of high school dropout and low levels of college attendance.[13]

To what extent are families implicated in these gaps? Or neighborhood conditions? Or the schools? These important questions are difficult to answer because such influences on academic development tend to be highly confounded in children's experience. Most children of privilege are privileged in all spheres of life: wealthy families usually live in good neighborhoods and send their children to good schools. At the other extreme is the other reality: the poor and nearly poor tend to live in distressed communities and attend resource-poor schools.

So how are we to understand the patterning of achievement differences across social lines? Families no doubt play a role. Children are learning all the time, in school and out, and in the primary grades especially, much of the school curriculum also is a home curriculum, as when parents work with their children on letter and number skills, reading, and so on. Parents of means generally did well in school themselves, and they have the tools to help their children do the same: they understand the skills and behaviors that lead to school success, exemplify them in family life, and are adept at cultivating them in their children. Low-income, low–socioeconomic status (SES) parents, on the other hand, often struggled at school, and many suffer low literacy levels. They generally want the same kinds of enriching experiences for their children as do well-off parents but lack the means to provide them.[14]

Such family differences are self-evidently relevant to children's school performance, and we could say the same for relevant school quality differences. But as a research objective, how can the effects of family poverty and children's schooling be isolated from one another and from other influences? This is where a seasonal perspective on learning can prove useful. Children are in their families and their neighborhoods year-round, but they are in school episodically. Schools play little or no role in children's learning during the summer months, and this holds especially when summer school is out of the picture, as is the case for the vast majority of children in the United States. The U.S. school-year calendar in this way approximates a natural experiment: with summer learning dependent on family and neighborhood conditions only, differences between school-year and summer learning *for the same children* isolate the role of schooling, with family and neighborhood conditions effectively held constant.

Heyns put this insight to good use in her Atlanta study, plotting school-year and summer achievement gains separately for black and white children and for children classified by family income level. Better-off children generally gained more than did disadvantaged children, but the gaps were uneven by season: relatively small during the school year, large during the summer months. In other words, poor children and black children came close to keeping up while in school, but during the summer, with learning dependent on home and community resources, they lagged far behind. On this basis, Heyns[15] concluded that schooling serves as compensatory education for disadvantaged children, helping build the academic skills missing from their out-of-school lives: "to some degree schooling is a surrogate for the parental influence common in middle class families."

This view of schooling finds support in numerous studies—both local[16] and national[17]—conducted since. Summer losses generally are greater in domains involving memorization (math computation, spelling) than conceptual understanding (math concepts or reasoning, reading comprehension) and larger in math than in the language arts. Synthesizing this literature, Harris Cooper and several colleagues found an average summer decline, across all grade levels and achievement areas, of approximately one month; comparing across-family SES or income groupings, the largest difference—on the order of three months—was in reading.[18] This review covers research through the mid-1990s, but more recent studies show a like pattern. Summarizing their methodologically sophisticated analyses of the Early Childhood Longitudinal Study (ECLS) data,[19] for example, Burkam and others concluded that children from higher-SES families learn more over the summer than do their less-advantaged counterparts.[20] Our own work with a sample of Baltimore school children paints a similar picture, but our Baltimore project also allows us to assess longer-term consequences of this pattern, something not done in other studies of differential summer learning. The sections that follow review this work.

## The Baltimore-based Beginning School Study and summer learning loss

For some years now, we have been extending the line of research initiated by Heyns. Our Baltimore project starts in first grade and tracks school progress through high school and into the years after (until age twenty-two). Having available fall and spring testing over the early project years, we compare school-year and summer achievement gains from the beginning of first grade through the end of elementary school (encompassing four summers), a longer time frame than other studies of school-year and summer learning. Having a first grade baseline is especially useful because it captures children's experience at the start of their formal schooling, the foundation for all later learning.[21] Our project also tracks long-term educational progress (until age twenty-two), allowing us to examine how achievement disparities from the early grades impact later school success, including high school dropout.

The setting for our research, Baltimore, Maryland, is a large deindustrializing East Coast city. Its population now, as it was when our project commenced in the early 1980s, is majority African American, and the city houses large pockets of concentrated poverty. In 1980, Baltimore's poverty rate for children younger than eighteen stood at 32 percent. Like conditions characterize Baltimore's public school system. In 1982, its enrollment was 77 percent African American (the figure now is 88 percent), and two-thirds qualified as low income according to guidelines for participation in the federal government's subsidized school meal program for needy children (now 83 percent qualify). In the early 1980s, the city's public school enrollment was in the vicinity of 120,000.[22] Owing to an exodus of middle-class families, the enrollment total now is just over 90,000.[23] This is the kind of urban school context where educational challenges run deep.

The Beginning School Study (BSS) panel consists of a representative random sample of Baltimore school children. The project began in fall 1982, when the study participants ($N = 790$), randomly selected from twenty public elementary schools within strata defined by school racial composition and socioeconomic level, were starting first grade. Their personal and academic development have been monitored almost continuously since (most recently in 2005–06 when 80 percent of the original group was interviewed), although the research summarized in this report stops at 1998, when most of the study participants were age twenty-two.[24]

To compute achievement gains on a seasonal basis requires twice-annual testing on the same children over at least two school years: fall to spring gains for the school year, and spring to fall for the summer months. During the 1982–83 school year, first grade for our study participants, the Baltimore City Public School System (BCPSS) administered the California Achievement Test (CAT) battery fall (October) and spring (May), and this testing schedule continued through the 1987–88 school year.[25] During this time, there was no mandatory summer school in Baltimore, and summer school attendance was exceedingly rare. This is advantageous for our purposes because summer school clouds interpretation of summer learning.

Although all 790 BSS participants were supposed to be captured in citywide testing, often the testing record is incomplete: for example, some children were absent on testing days, some testing data were lost, and most children who transferred to another school system were not covered after they left. However, our checking reveals no substantial skews or bias owing to these and other sources of panel attrition.[26]

All our studies in this area use two subtests from the CAT battery: Reading Comprehension (CAT-R) and Mathematics Concepts and Applications (CAT-M), testing domains included in all forms of the CAT battery through twelfth grade and ones less subject to ceiling constraints than some of the other CAT subtests.[27] As mentioned, summer learning losses tend to be more pronounced for quantitative skills than for verbal (the interpretation being that quantitative skills are less likely to be learned at home) and for skills that are learned through practice and drill, as opposed to more conceptually based skill areas (the interpretation being that the former are more prone to forgetting without practice). That being the case, these two subtests may understate summer learning losses and so very likely afford a conservative picture. The overview that follows focuses on results for Reading Comprehension, as those for math are virtually identical.

Figure 1.1 fairly captures the key details of summer and winter learning patterns in the BSS. We have reported more refined statistical analyses also,[28] but the picture is the same. The graphs show the timeline of achievement gains, by season, for the five elementary school years separately for children classified as "high" and "low" according to family socioeconomic standing.

Because Baltimore's public schools serve mainly low-income students, half the BSS panel is in the low-SES group, and roughly a fourth is in the high group, based on parents' education, parents' job status, and family income. A middle group, not included in this display, makes up the remaining fourth of the panel. Their results generally fall between the two extremes.[29] The SES classification provides good discrimination: for example, mothers' education averages 10.0 years for the lowest-SES group, 12.0 years for the middle group, and 14.6 years for the highest group.[30]

Season-specific Reading Comprehension gains are reported *cumulatively* across years. The second school-year gain adds onto the first, the third onto the second, and so forth through all five school years. Likewise with summer gains, although there is one less summer: five school years bracket four summers. Figure 1.1 shows essentially no disparity across social lines in achievement gains during the school year, revealing that disadvantaged children

**Figure 1.1. Summer and winter learning patterns of disadvantaged versus better-off Baltimore schoolchildren**

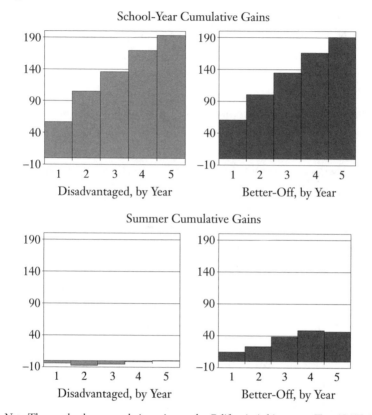

School-Year Cumulative Gains

Disadvantaged, by Year                Better-Off, by Year

Summer Cumulative Gains

Disadvantaged, by Year                Better-Off, by Year

*Note:* The graphs show cumulative gains on the California Achievement Test (CAT) in reading over elementary school years and summers. The sample consists of Baltimore public school students who entered first grade in 1982. Test "scale scores" are CAT scores calibrated to measure growth over a student's twelve-year school career.

*Source:* Entwisle, Alexander, and Olson (1977), Table 3.1.

in Baltimore pretty well keep up with their more advantaged peers *while they are in school.* In fact, they might even make up a bit of ground: their cumulative school-year gain is 191.3 points, and that for the high-SES group is 187.0 points.[31]

Such parity hardly accords with popular (and some professional) depictions of poor children's schooling, and it suggests that something unexpected is happening in Baltimore. But not just in Baltimore because like results have been reported for other cities[32] and in national data.[33] These studies do not all show school-year parity, as in the BSS, but they all show much smaller achievement gap disparities during the school year than during the summer months, and indeed, it is the seasonal contrast, to which we now turn, that fills out the picture.

Poor children in Baltimore may be progressing in parallel with better-off children during the school year, but that does not mean they are performing at the same level at year's end. To the contrary, at the end of elementary school, they lag far behind, which we attribute to two sources: they start school already behind, a deficit that their good school-year gains do not erase;[34] and during the summer, when they are cut off from the school's resources, they lose ground relative to higher-SES children. These summer differentials are displayed in the right pair of graphs in Figure 1.1.

During the summer months over the elementary school years, disadvantaged children essentially tread water: they gain a few points some summers and lose a few in others, a pattern we call "summer slide." The BSS children who are most well off, in contrast, make consistent summer gains. They register a total gain across all four summers of fifty-two CAT-R points, *a large enough difference to account for almost all the increase in the achievement gap across social lines registered during the elementary school years.* So, indeed, the achievement gap widens over time, but driving this widening are resource disparities in children's lives *outside school*, something only evident when viewed through the powerful lens of seasonal comparisons.

Figure 1.1 also establishes that children—all children—learn more when in school than when not in school, and it suggests that the first two summers may be critical times for the retention of basic skills because that is when we see the largest gain differences. (Keep in mind that our focus is the primary grades and foundational academic skills.) Comparisons across skill domains also may identify areas of particular concern. Consistent with the idea that math learning in the early grades is less often practiced at home and hence more school dependent, other BSS analyses show smaller summer gains altogether and greater losses in math than in reading.[35] Unfortunately, BSS studies are not able to inform like questions about skills that are more drill-dependent as opposed to conceptual because this important question requires a broader sampling of achievement domains.

_____

## *Of what consequence are summer learning differentials?*

Studies of the seasonality of learning do not line up perfectly. They differ from one another in many ways, including population coverage, locality, grade-level coverage, assessment instruments, skill domains, the social comparisons made, and exactly how those social distinctions are measured. Results differ, too, but the general pattern seen in the BSS is fairly representative, and for us, one fact stands out: disadvantaged children come closer to keeping up during the school year than they do during the summer months.

It seems self-evident that a large summer gap in cognitive skill development over the early years of children's schooling will have long-term repercussions, yet there is no research to date explicitly focused on consequences. Studies instead have centered on the pattern itself—making sure it is well documented—and to a lesser extent on identifying summer experiences that can account for summer learning differences (library usage, for example). Still, we know that cognitive assessments tend to be moderately to highly correlated over time, usually in the vicinity of 0.5 to 0.6.[36] This being the case, low achievement in the elementary grades often will translate into low achievement later and so indirectly impact educational opportunities and placements in the upper grades that select on level of academic performance, like high school curriculum placement.

A like line of reasoning suggests that achievement differences across social lines will influence differences across social lines in other areas of schooling. And now we know, as reviewed in the previous section, that achievement differences by family background over the early years largely derive from home and neighborhood conditions. This achievement shortfall during the elementary school years likely casts a long shadow. A recent BSS analysis reports evidence to that effect in three areas: curricular track placement in high school, high school dropout, and college attendance.[37] We review that work next.

The BCPSS discontinued use of the CAT battery after BSS project year 8, and in years 7 and 8, testing was done in the spring only, which means the partitioning of gains by season cannot be done for those years. However, beginning in the spring of project year 9, the first year of high school for those promoted regularly each year, the BSS did its own administration of the CAT-R and CAT-M subtests, achieving 75 percent panel coverage.[38]

The beginning of high school is a critical time in the schooling process. Among other considerations, it is when serious preparation for college begins, and we know academic difficulties during that period cause problems later.[39] In year 9, the low-SES group's Reading Comprehension average lagged seventy-three points behind the high-SES group's, a large difference of roughly 0.88 SD (referenced to the standard deviation for high- and low-SES youth combined). Research at the high school level usually takes such differences as "given," but because the BSS includes a detailed testing history back to first grade, we can see how that ninth-grade difference builds up over the years. Doing so proves an interesting exercise.

About a third of the difference, 26.5 points, was in place in the fall of 1982 when these children started first grade: an achievement gap "at the starting gate."[40] With kindergarten now nearly universal (in the early 1980s, when the BSS began, kindergarten was not yet mandatory in Baltimore) and preschool education common, it cannot be said that first grade represents children's first encounter with formal schooling, but it seems safe to credit the bulk of this difference to experiences and resources outside school that predate school entry.[41]

The remaining two-thirds of the year 9 achievement gap originates over the elementary and middle school years, with the largest single component, 48.5 points, being the cumulative summer learning gap from the five elementary years. The school-year contributions over those same years, in comparison, are trivially small: the low-SES group actually gains a bit more in elementary school than does the high group (5.2 points, not a significant difference), but over years 6 though 9, they again lose ground by some three points (for school years and summers combined, also not significant).

According to this partitioning, then, children's lives *outside school* over the preschool years and during the elementary grades account for almost all of the achievement gap that separates low- and high-SES children at the start of high school. Both groups learn a great deal more while in school than during the summer months—we do not want to lose sight of that (see Figure 1.1)—but it is during the summer months specifically that the higher-SES group forges ahead. Indeed, summers account for *most* of the higher-SES group's achievement advantage at the start of high school.

What, then, are some of the practical consequences of this? Sixty-two percent of the high-SES group was enrolled in a college preparatory program in high school versus just 13 percent of low-SES youth, a forty-nine-point difference. The latter, in addition, was more likely to enter adulthood without high school certification (36 percent versus 3 percent at age twenty-two) and less likely to attend a four-year college (7 percent versus 59 percent, also at age twenty-two). It is certain that the two groups' respective achievement levels as ninth graders contributed in some measure to all three disparities. Our goal was to explore the role played specifically by summer learning differences.

High school curriculum over the high school years was determined from information on the type of school attended (that is, citywide academic magnet, citywide vocational magnet, zoned comprehensive) and student self-reports. Here we distinguish academic (or college preparatory) students from general program and vocational program students based on their last known or most recent program before graduation. The low-SES, noncollege-track group's year 9 CAT-R average lags 116 points behind that of the high-SES, college-track group's, a difference of 1.3 SD. It hardly surprises that high schoolers in the college-bound program are more academically accomplished, but the origins of their 116-point advantage might surprise: 40 points from the fall of first grade, an 8-point cumulative school-year disadvantage over school years 1 through 5 (the elementary years), an extraordinary 76-point cumulative summer advantage over the elementary years (four summers for five school years), and a mere 7-point advantage over years 6 through 9 (years for which we cannot separate the school-year and summer components).

No doubt college prep students' superior CAT scores figured prominently in their high school program placement. In a school system where 40 percent of students leave high school without degrees,[42] degree attainment is a noteworthy accomplishment. These pupils, on the whole, were much better qualified than those placed in general and vocational programs, but the bulk of their year 9 CAT-R advantage—more than half—reflects differential gains over the summer months during the elementary grades. These youngsters do have an advantage—a substantial one—but in the main, it is a family advantage, not a school advantage.

The picture is much the same later. In 1997–98, roughly four years after the panel's "on-time" high school graduation in spring 1994, 80 percent of the original group was reinterviewed. The survey asked about high school completion and college attendance, among other things. Looking at the extremes of schooling, there is a huge 133-point difference (1.4 SD) between the year 9 cognitive scores of low-SES permanent high school dropouts (those who at age twenty-two lack high school certification of any sort, including the GED) and of high-SES panel members who attended four-year colleges in pursuit of a bachelor's degree. Those 133 points are grounded in a 43-point high-SES advantage from the fall of first grade, a 3-point deficit in their school-year gains over the elementary years, an 87-point advantage in summer gains over the elementary years, and a 7-point advantage over years 6 through 9.

These figures make it hard to escape the conclusion that lower-SES children's CAT-R shortfall during periods of school nonattendance earlier in their lives leads to lower levels of educational accomplishment in young adulthood. Just as with high school curriculum placements, we observe tangible adverse educational consequences for disadvantaged children, mediated through early patterns of cognitive development that trace back to their lives outside school.[43]

## *Implications*

This line of research has generated considerable interest in recent years, especially among those who advocate redirecting parts of the summer break to academic pursuits—for example, proponents of summer school as an alternative to the twin evils of social promotion and grade retention[44] and advocates for calendar reform along the lines of year-round schooling.[45] The finding that disadvantaged children slip back relative to better-off children when not in school helps make the case for useful alternatives to the long summer void—that is, if some school is good, more school should be better. Assuming the summer programming is well considered, we think the case a compelling one.

It is now well established that cognitive abilities are enhanced by schooling.[46] Ceci reviews evidence from eight relevant literatures, with studies of summer learning loss one of the eight.[47] Others include research on the correlation between IQ and years in school (for example, comparing changes in the scores of high school dropouts after they left school with those of similar students who remained in school), effects of delayed school beginning, early termination, and intermittent school attendance (owing to war and natural disasters, for example) on IQ, and age or cohort differences in relation to IQ (for example, comparing the scores of children who are of like age—perhaps a month apart—but in different grades owing to age cutoffs for starting kindergarten or first grade). Of the summer learning literature, Ceci says: "The most basic example of the impact of schooling on IQ performance can be found in the small but reliable decrement in IQ during the summer vacation, especially among low-income youngsters whose summer activities are least likely to resemble those found in school."[48]

Ceci's point is an astute one: school-like activities are needed for low-income children's scores to improve, and they, more than other children, depend on the schools to provide them. If low-income children in fact come closer to keeping up during the school year, as the accumulated evidence indicates, then schools surely are implicated, and those of us who care about these children's well-being ought to ponder how those benefits can be extended beyond the traditional school day. After-school programming, summer programming, and modified calendars are the obvious options.[49] The family's role in summer learning also needs to be better understood,[50] but here we focus on school-like interventions for which BSS and related research have a number of clear implications.

With most of the achievement gap increase early in elementary school, that is where corrective interventions should be targeted, or even before. To catch up, children who are behind academically need to make larger-than-average gains, which is expecting a great deal of struggling students. Accordingly, a high priority should be to keep the achievement gap from opening wide in the first place. The earlier we can intervene—with the kinds of preschool compensatory education initiatives that have proved effective—the better.[51]

Quality preschool and full-day kindergarten programs[52] can reduce the achievement gap associated with SES when children start first grade, but to help them keep up later will require extra resources and enrichment experiences on an ongoing basis. Disadvantaged children need year-round supplemental programming to counter the continuing press of family and community conditions that hold them back, which leads us to support summer school or extended-year programs targeted specifically for poor children, as well as supplemental school-year services for these children during the early grades.

The Chicago Longitudinal Study shows that intense supplementation of learning resources in the early grades helps poor children maintain the academic edge they get from attending a good preschool *and* that these benefits then continue into the upper grades.[53] An important finding of the Chicago study was that preschool and school-year supplementation was most effective in combination, one building on the other.

The Chicago intervention is not a summer program, but it seems reasonable that summer enrichment programs specifically for disadvantaged students before and after first grade would confer similar, if not greater, benefits. But how should these summer programs be designed? Certainly not like summer programs of the past because these magnify, not shrink, disparities across socioeconomic lines.[54] This is a general concern with so-called universal programs. With the playing field uneven and parents of means able to find their way to higher-quality programs (and their children better positioned to profit from educationally enriching experiences), all children may see their skills improve, but those who are better off to begin with often gain more (another instance of the rich getting richer). In this way, well-intentioned and effective interventions can have the perverse effect of exacerbating the achievement gap across social lines.[55] This is why we support programs targeted for disadvantaged children specifically.

A strong curriculum comes first, one that is focused on reading because reading is the foundation for all that follows. Heyns found reading to be the single summer activity most strongly and consistently related to summer learning, whether measured by the number of books read, the time spent reading, or the regularity of library use.[56] Reading during the summer increased children's vocabulary test scores and had a substantial effect on achievement largely independent of family background. Likewise, in the BSS, children's use of the library in summer, especially taking out books, predicts summer gains in achievement. Educational policies that increase access to books, perhaps through increased library services, stand to have an important impact on achievement, particularly for less-advantaged children.

But summer schools should not be limited to traditional academics. In the BSS, we find that better-off children more often go to city and state parks, fairs or carnivals, and take day or overnight trips. They also more often take swimming, dance, and music lessons; visit local parks, museums, science centers, and zoos; and make more visits to the library in summer. In addition, children living in better neighborhoods play more organized sports in summer, which can reap dividends in unexpected ways. Sports like soccer, field hockey, and softball obligate children to learn complicated rule systems, encourage children to work together toward shared goals, and may stimulate interest in topics like batting percentages, odds of winning or losing, and so on. These and other like activities support engaged learning outside the traditional classroom setting, and as instances of incidental learning, they can spill over to formal academics.[57]

Building on such leads, summer programs for disadvantaged children should supplement academics with heavy doses of physical activity and enrichment experiences. Such an expanded agenda is important for another reason also: to make summer school fun. To realize their potential, summer programs should be engaging and nonpunitive. For many disadvantaged, poor-performing children, *school* is synonymous with *failure*; for them, school is punishing, not fun. Owing to their coercive cast, mandatory programs for children who fall short of promotion guidelines no doubt face a particular challenge in transforming the experience.

These suggestions highlight the need to supplement regular schooling through a long-term coordinated program of interventions embodying best-practice principles.[58] Such programs will need to begin as early as age three and continue thereafter in a sustained way. And even then, because the obstacles are daunting, "reasonable progress" ought to be the realistic expectation: there are no certain solutions to overcoming the drag of poverty and distressed neighborhood conditions. But seasonal studies of learning patterns establish that most children are capable learners, and there can be little question that the vast majority of struggling students have the ability to master the early school curriculum at a reasonable level of proficiency. We know a great deal about how to help these children succeed academically, more than generally is realized. The question now is how aggressively we will work at putting that knowledge to use.

### Notes

1. Gold, K. M. (2002). *School's in: The history of summer education in American public schools*. New York: Lang; Weiss, J., & Brown, R. S. (2003). Telling tales over time: Constructing and deconstructing the school calendar. *Teachers College Record, 105*(9).

2. Barrett, M. (1990, November). The case for more school days. *Atlantic Monthly*. Retrieved October 12, 1999, from http://www.theatlantic.com.

3. U.S. Department of Education. (2002). *Digest of education statistics, 2002*. Washington, DC: U.S. Department of Education, National Center for Education Statistics.

4. White, K. (1999, October 27). Quietly, the school calendar evolves. *Education Week*. Retrieved August 26, 2004, from http://www.edweek.org/ew/index.html.

5. Borman, G. D. (2001). Summers are for learning. *Principal, 80*(3), 26–29.

6. Heyns, B. (1978). *Summer learning and the effects of schooling*. Orlando, FL: Academic Press.

7. McCabe, M. (2004, January 27). Year-round schooling. *Education Week on the Web*. Retrieved November 20, 2006, from http://www.edweek.org/ew/index.html.

8. Hofferth, S. L., Shauman, K. A., Henke, R. R., & West, J. (1998). *Characteristics of children's early care and education programs: Data from the 1995 National Household Education Survey*. Washington, DC: U.S. Department of Education, National Center for Education Statistics. P. 42.

9. Current summer enrollments very likely are well above the 1996 level but still the exception. According to data from the Bureau of Labor Statistics (Stringer, T. [2002-03, Winter]. Summertime, summer teens: Summer school enrollment and the youth labor force. *Occupational Outlook Quarterly, 46*[4], 36–51), in July 2002 just under 35 percent of youth in the sixteen- to nineteen-year age bracket was enrolled in summer programs, representing an increase from under 20 percent in 1994. But that age range extends beyond the K–12 population, and what counts as "summer school enrollment" is not defined. The cited 1996 report shows 14.9 percent of eleventh and twelfth graders attending summer school, a much smaller figure than the 1994 Bureau of Labor Statistics figure for all youth aged sixteen to nineteen; for grades 1 through 7, the 1996 summer enrollment was just 7.5 percent.

10. Cooper, H., Nye, B., Charlton, K., Lindsay, J., & Greathouse, S. (1996). The effects of summer vacation on achievement test scores: A narrative and meta-analytic review. *Review of Educational Research, 66*(3), 227–268.

11. Heyns. (1978).

12. Phillips, M., Crouse, J., & Ralph, J. (1998). Does the black-white test score gap widen after children enter school? In C. Jencks & M. Phillips (Eds.), *The black-white test score gap* (pp. 229–272). Washington, DC: Brookings.

13. Entwisle, D. R., Alexander, K. L., & Olson, L. S. (1997). *Children, schools and inequality*. Boulder, CO: Westview Press. Table 7.21.

14. Chin, T., & Phillips, M. (2004, July). Social reproduction and child-rearing practices: Social class, children's agency, and the summer activity gap. *Sociology of Education, 77*, 185–210.

15. Heyns. (1978). P. 188.

16. Murnane, R. J. (1975). *The impact of school resources on the learning of inner city children*. Cambridge, MA: Ballinger.

17. Downey, D. B., von Hippel, P. T., & Broh, B. (2004). Are schools the great equalizer? Cognitive inequality during the summer months and the school year. *American Sociological Review, 69*(5), 613–635; Burkam, D. T., Ready, D. D., Lee, V. E., & LoGerfo, L. F. (2004, January). Social-class differences in summer learning between kindergarten and first grade: Model specification and estimation. *Sociology of Education, 77*, 1–31.

18. Cooper et al. (1996).

19. The Early Childhood Longitudinal Study tracks achievement over kindergarten, first grade, and the summer for a national sample of children who began kindergarten in the fall of 1998.

20. Burkam et al. (2004).

21. Entwisle, D. R., & Alexander, K. L. (1989). Early schooling as a "critical period" phenomenon. In K. Namboodiri & R. Corwin (Eds.), *Sociology of education and socialization* (pp. 27–55). Greenwich, CT: JAI Press; Entwisle, D. R., & Alexander, K. L. (1993). Entry into schools: The beginning school transition and educational stratification in the United States. *Annual Review of Sociology 19*, 401–423.

22. Bowler, M. (1991). *The lessons of change: Baltimore schools in the modern era.* Baltimore: Fund for Educational Excellence. P. 43.

23. Maryland State Department of Education. (2004). *The fact book, 2003–2004.* Baltimore: Author.

24. Entwisle, Alexander, & Olson. (1997).

25. Testing was *not done* on the first day of class in the fall or the last day in the spring. Accordingly, the interval between tests does not accurately bracket either the summer or the school year, and spring-to-fall differences include some in-school time. This is a source of inaccuracy shared by practically all studies in this literature; however, a recent study by Burkam et al. (2004) uses exact testing dates and school opening and closing dates to calculate true summer gains and losses. In that analysis, the basic pattern of summer learning differences across social lines is robust, even after adjustment for these measurement inaccuracies.

26. Entwisle, Alexander, & Olson. (1997). Appendix A.

27. Ceiling constraints can distort results. If a student answers all questions correctly, he or she might have scored even higher on a more sensitive test. This is a particular problem for research on the achievement gap because it would dampen high–low income differences (for example, if more upper-income than lower-income students score at the ceiling, as would be expected).

28. Alexander, K. L., Entwisle, D. R., & Olson, L. S. (2001). Schools, achievement and inequality: A seasonal perspective. *Educational Evaluation and Policy Analysis, 23*(2), 171–191.

29. All socioeconomic status data are reported by parents, except family income (low, not low), which is from school records indicating participation in the federal government's meal subsidy program for low-income families.

30. "Highest" should be understood as relative to Baltimore's public school enrollment, which includes few genuinely wealthy families.

31. CAT scale scores are reported. These are vertically calibrated across versions of the CAT battery designed for administration at different grade levels, approximating a single continuum of performance across all points of comparison. However, the CAT distribution lacks a meaningful zero point—that is, the lowest possible score on the fall first-grade CAT-R subtest is 133.

32. Heyns. (1978); Murnane. (1975).

33. Heyns, B. (1987). Schooling and cognitive development: Is there a season for learning? *Child Development, 58*(5), 1151–1160; Downey, von Hippel, & Broh. (2004).

34. In our data, the high–low SES CAT-R difference in the fall of first grade is twenty-seven scale points, or roughly 0.7 SD.

35. Alexander, Entwisle, & Olson. (2001); Entwisle, D. R., & Alexander, K. L. (1992). Summer setback: Race, poverty, school composition, and mathematics achievement in the first two years of school. *American Sociological Review, 57*(1), 72–84; Entwisle, D. R., & Alexander, K. L. (1994). Winter setback: School racial composition and learning to read. *American Sociological Review, 59*(3), 446–460; Entwisle, Alexander, & Olson. (1997).

36. Entwisle, Alexander, & Olson. (1997). Table 7.21.

37. Alexander, K. L., Entwisle, D. R., & Olson, L. S. (2007). Lasting consequences of the summer learning gap. *American Sociological Review, 72,* 167–180.

38. Testing continued for roughly eighteen months. Scores are referenced back to the spring of year 9 using a linear interpolation. In analyses using these data, missing data for cases not covered and for earlier gaps in the testing record were estimated using multiple imputation methods (Allison, P. D. [2002]. *Missing data.* Thousand Oaks, CA: Sage). Imputed and nonimputed results are close, but for consistency here, we review results using the imputed data.

39. Roderick, M., & Camburn, E. (1999). Risk and recovery from course failure in the early years of high school. *American Educational Research Journal, 36*(2), 303–343.

40. Lee, V. E., & Burkam, D. T. (2002). *Inequality at the starting gate.* Washington, DC: Economic Policy Institute.

41. We say this because many children even today still attend just half-day kindergarten (45 percent in the late 1990s) (West, J., Denton, K., & Reaney, L. M. [2001]. *The kindergarten year: Findings from the Early Childhood Longitudinal Study.* Washington, DC: National Center for Educational Statistics), and kindergarten often stresses social skills over academic learning. Also, although children's achievement levels do improve over the kindergarten year, they do so at a slower rate than in first grade (Downey, von Hippel, & Broh, 2004).

42. Alexander, K. L., Entwisle, D. R., & Horsey, C. (1997). From first grade forward: Early foundations of high school dropout. *Sociology of Education, 70*(2), 87–107; Alexander, K. L., Entwisle, D. R., & Kabbani, N. (2001). The dropout process in life course perspective: Early risk factors at home and school. *Teachers College Record, 103*(5), 760–822.

43. These are extreme comparisons to make the point, but formal analyses with the entire BSS panel show the same pattern.

44. Alexander, K. L., Entwisle, D. R., & Kabbani, N. (2003). Grade retention, social promotion, and "third way" alternatives. In A. J. Reynolds, M. C. Wang, & H. J. Walberg (Eds.), *Early childhood programs for a new century* (pp. 197–238). Washington, DC: Child Welfare League of America.

45. Ballinger, C. (2004). Why wait for summer? Quicker intervention, better results. In G. D. Borman & M. Boulay (Eds.), *Summer learning: Research, policies, and programs* (pp. 279–284). Mahwah, NJ: Erlbaum; Cooper, H. (2004). Is the school calendar dated? Education, economics, and the politics of time. In G. D. Borman & M. Boulay (Eds.), *Summer learning: Research, policies, and programs* (pp. 3–23). Mahwah, NJ: Erlbaum; White. (1999).

46. Winship, C., & Korenman, S. (1997). Does staying in school make you smarter? The effect of education on IQ in *The Bell Curve*. In B. Devlin, S. E. Fienberg, D. Resnick, & K. Roeder (Eds.), *Intelligence and success: Is it all in the genes? Scientists respond to The Bell Curve* (pp. 245–265). New York: Springer-Verlag.

47. Ceci, S. J. (1991). How much does schooling influence general intelligence and its cognitive components? A reassessment of the evidence. *Developmental Psychology, 27*(5), 703–722.

48. Ceci. (1991). P. 705.

49. Lauer, P. A., Akiba, M., Wilkerson, S. B., Apthorp, H. S., Snow, D., & Martin-Glenn, M. L. (2006). Out-of-school-time programs: A meta-analysis of effects for at-risk students. *Review of Educational Research, 76*(2), 275–313; Cooper. (2004).

50. Entwisle, D. R., Alexander, K. L., & Olson, L. S. (2000). Summer learning and home environment. In R. D. Kahlenberg (Ed.), *A notion at risk: Preserving public education as an engine for social mobility* (pp. 9–30). New York: Century Foundation Press; Entwisle, D. R., Alexander, K. L., & Olson, L. S. (2001, Fall). Keep the faucet flowing: Summer learning and home environment. *American Educator, 25*(3), 10–15, 47.

51. Ramey, C. T., Campbell, F. A., & Blair, C. (1998). Enhancing the life course for high-risk children: Results from the Abecedarian Project. In J. Crane (Ed.), *Social programs that work* (pp. 163–183). New York: Russell Sage Foundation; Schweinhart, L. J., & Weikart, D. P. (1998). High/Scope Perry Preschool Program effects at age twenty-seven. In J. Crane (Ed.), *Social programs that work* (pp. 148–183). New York: Russell Sage Foundation; Reynolds, A. J., & Temple, J. A. (1998). Extended early childhood intervention and school achievement: Age thirteen findings from the Chicago Longitudinal Study. *Child Development, 69*(1), 231–246.

52. Cryan, J., Sheehan, R., Weichel, J., & Bandy-Hedden, I. G. (1992). Success outcomes of full-day kindergarten: More positive behavior and increased achievement in the years after. *Early Childhood Research Quarterly, 7*(2), 187–203; Entwisle, D. R., Alexander, K. L., Cadigan, D., & Pallas, A. M. (1987). Kindergarten experience: Cognitive effects or socialization? *American Educational Research Journal, 24*(3), 337–364; Karweit, N. (1989). Effective kindergarten practices for students at risk. In R. E. Slavin, N. L. Karweit, & N. A. Madden (Eds.), *Effective programs for students at risk* (pp. 103–142). Needham Heights, MA: Allyn & Bacon.

53. Reynolds, A. J. (1994). Effects of a preschool plus follow-on intervention for children at risk. *Developmental Psychology, 30*(6), 787–804; Reynolds & Temple. (1998); Temple, J. A., Reynolds, A. J., & Miedel, W. T. (1998). *Can early intervention prevent high school dropout? Evidence from the Chicago Child-Parent Center.* Madison: University of Wisconsin, Institute for Research on Poverty.

54. Cooper, H., Charlton, K., Valentine, J. C., & Muhlenbruck, L. (2000). *Making the most of summer school: A meta-analytic and narrative review. Monograph Series for the Society for Research in Child Development, 65*(1, Serial No. 260); Entwisle, D. R., Alexander, K. L., & Olson, L. S. (2000). Summer learning and home environment. In R. D. Kahlenberg (Ed.), *A notion at risk:*

*Preserving public education as an engine for social mobility* (pp. 9–30). New York: Century Foundation Press; Heyns. (1978).

55. Ceci, S. J., & Papierno, P. B. (2005, March). The rhetoric and reality of gap closing. When the "have-nots" gain but the "haves" gain even more. *American Psychologist, 60*(2), 149–160.

56. Heyns. (1978).

57. For a discussion of the link between organized sports and academic progress, see Entwisle, D. R., Alexander, K. L., & Olson, L. S. (1994, December). The gender gap in math: Its possible origins in neighborhood effects. *American Sociological Review, 59*, 822–838.

58. Borman, G. D., & Dowling, N. (2006). The longitudinal achievement effects of multi-year summer school: Evidence from the Teach Baltimore randomized field trial. *Educational Evaluation and Policy Analysis, 28*(1), 25–48; Cooper et al. (2000); Lauer et al. (2006).

KARL L. ALEXANDER *is John Dewey Professor of Sociology and chair of the Department of Sociology at the Johns Hopkins University in Baltimore, Maryland.*

DORIS R. ENTWISLE *is research professor of sociology at the Johns Hopkins University.*

LINDA STEFFEL OLSON *is associate research scientist in the Department of Sociology at the Johns Hopkins University.*

*Children are more vulnerable to gaining body mass index during the summer than during the school year, suggesting that schools help to reduce childhood obesity.*

# 2

# Childhood body mass index gain during the summer versus during the school year

*Douglas B. Downey, Heather R. Boughton*

BY NOW IT IS WELL KNOWN that obesity has been increasing in the United States. Whereas this health problem has affected nearly every segment of the population, the impact on children, in whom the incidence of obesity has tripled in the last twenty years, is of special note.[1] Overweight children tend to become overweight adults, more vulnerable to the wide range of health problems associated with obesity. The role that schools play in this problem is difficult to discern, however, because children's health is affected by both school and nonschool factors. In this chapter, we discuss innovative research that compares children's body mass index (BMI) gains in the summer versus the school year. Although many scholars, and certainly the popular media, currently focus on school-based solutions to childhood obesity, this research suggests that when it comes to children's BMI gain, schools are more a part of the solution than the problem. Specifically, children gain BMI roughly twice as fast during the summer as during the school year.

NEW DIRECTIONS FOR YOUTH DEVELOPMENT, NO. 114, SUMMER 2007 © WILEY PERIODICALS, INC.
Published online in Wiley InterScience (www.interscience.wiley.com) • DOI: 10.1002/yd.211

The growth of childhood obesity in the United States is an example of C. Wright Mills's distinction between "public issues" and "private troubles."[2] If a modest number of children are obese, then we might properly ask, "How differently are they conducting their lives than other children?" Obesity is a "private trouble" for this small group. But when a large and increasing percentage of the population becomes obese, then the problem is no longer readily understood as the private troubles of individuals. Something about the opportunity to become obese itself has changed. Certainly the consequences of greater obesity, in terms of its costs, have become a public issue. Accordingly, to understand the increase in childhood obesity and the policies that might arrest its growth, the proper focus is on societal-level factors.

Schools are an obvious societal-level culprit for many reasons. After the family, schools are arguably the most critical socializing agent in children's lives. Despite the growth in home schooling and private schools, the percentage of children attending public schools has remained at about 90 percent for several decades.[3] Because they serve so many children and play such an important role in children's lives, schools have been the obvious institution through which the public interest in children's health has been administered. For example, in most states children are required to receive common vaccinations before entering their first year of formal schooling. It is no surprise that policymakers and researchers alike have directed so much attention toward understanding how schools have contributed to childhood obesity.

But is this emphasis on schools appropriate? School critics argue that schools expose children to too much unhealthy food and not enough exercise, thereby contributing to the rapid increase in the prevalence of childhood obesity.[4] Consequently, a number of school districts have banned soda machines while others have made serious changes to school lunches, long known for their poor nutrition. Arkansas has initiated a program where parents are informed not only of their children's academic performance but also of their BMI. If a child is overweight, the parents receive a letter suggesting changes in diet and activity level and encouraging the parents to discuss the child's situation further with a physician.[5]

Some researchers, however, maintain that factors located outside schools are to blame for these increasing rates; this camp focuses on excessive fast-food consumption and television watching,[6] among other factors, as responsible for childhood obesity. One reason for suspecting that schools may not be the wrongdoer they are made out to be is that children spend surprisingly little time at school. The average eighteen-year-old American has spent just 13 percent of his or her waking time in school.[7] Furthermore, there is considerable evidence that factors such as neighborhood characteristics[8] and family socioeconomic status[9] influence a wide range of children's health issues. With so many other environmental factors influencing children's health, precisely what role schools play is an open question.

Properly identifying how schools affect children's obesity presents a challenge for researchers because children's BMI is influenced both by school factors (for example, lunch quality, physical education classes) and also by nonschool factors (family eating and exercise habits, access to recreational facilities). Below we describe how researchers have employed seasonal comparisons, contrasting what happens during the school year with that during the summer, as an analytic tool for separating school and nonschool effects. Most seasonal comparisons have focused on children's gains in math and reading skills, which we describe first, but recently scholars have extended this approach to children's BMI gains.

## Logic and promise of seasonal comparisons

Understanding how schools matter requires knowing how things would turn out if children were not in school. Because most children attend school on a seasonal basis—beginning in the fall and ending in the spring—it is possible to compare their growth during the school year with that observed in the summer. Heyns articulated the usefulness of this comparison by conceptualizing the growth rate during the summer as solely a function of nonschool-related factors (family, neighborhood), while the growth rate during the school year is a function of these same nonschool factors and school factors (teacher and administrator quality).[10] Assuming that the nonschool factors that influence children do not change in a dramatic way from season to season,[11] the simple difference between school-year growth and summer growth represents a clever estimate of the school effect, independent of nonschool factors.[12]

Using this seasonal approach, researchers have documented how inequality in children's math and reading skills tends to grow faster in the summer than during the school year.[13] Surprisingly, children of low- and those of high-socioeconomic status (SES) learn at roughly similar rates during the school year. But during the summer, high-SES children continue to make gains, albeit modest ones, whereas low-SES children often lose skills, what Entwisle and Alexander termed "summer setback."[14] This provocative pattern has been demonstrated in local samples in Atlanta[15] and Baltimore[16] and, more recently, replicated in a national sample of young elementary school children.[17] Despite considerable differences in quality, schools tend to reduce the level of inequality we observe in their absence.

One reason this is so important is that it compels us to rethink a claim attractive to many critics of the education system: that schools play a pernicious role in society by providing dramatically unequal opportunities to children.[18] Instead, seasonal comparison research suggests that disadvantaged children enjoy a greater benefit from schooling than advantaged children.

Of course, this conclusion is puzzling given that schools serving advantaged children typically enjoy better teachers and more resources than schools serving disadvantaged children.[19] Our explanation is that although these disparities in school quality are real and meaningful, they are more modest than the differences in children's nonschool environments. As a result, children from extremely poor families can attend poor schools and still enjoy a more substantial "school boost" than children from advantaged families attending the best schools (Figure 2.1).

NEW DIRECTIONS FOR YOUTH DEVELOPMENT • DOI: 10.1002/yd

**Figure 2.1. How unequal schools equalize**

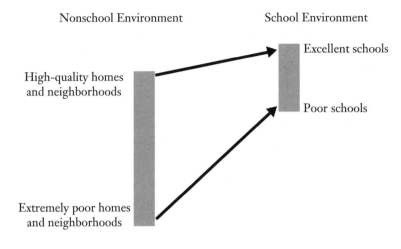

More recently, Downey, von Hippel, and Hughes have employed the seasonal comparison approach as a way to identify high-quality schools.[20] Because children's performances on standardized tests are influenced by a mixture of both school and nonschool factors, methods of evaluating schools that ignore variations in non-school environments are biased. To address this problem, the authors evaluated schools through what they call "impact," the difference in children's learning rates between the summer and the school year, and concluded that our ideas about which schools are "failing" change in an important way when we account for children's varying nonschool environments.[21] By using seasonal comparisons to more persuasively estimate the actual school effect, the impact measure provides a more accurate, and alarmingly different, way of gauging school quality.

Seasonal comparison work is admittedly rare, in part because it requires data collected at the beginning and end of the school year rather than annually. To date, it has been applied primarily to cognitive skills outcomes, but recently scholars have extended this approach to studying children's BMI gain as a way of assessing how schools influence childhood obesity.

## Seasonal comparisons and children's BMI

Employing seasonal comparisons as a way to understand school-ing's role in childhood obesity is especially attractive given that chil-dren's BMI gains are affected by both school and nonschool factors. One way of gaining leverage on schools' causal role is to consider the counterfactual, "What would BMI gain look like if children were not attending school?" A preferred way of answering this question would be to randomly assign children to school and non-school conditions and then compare the two groups' BMI gains over time. The power of random assignment would provide us with confidence that differences between groups were likely a result of the school "treatment."

Of course, few parents would agree to have their child assigned to a "nonschool" condition, and so seasonal comparisons offer a practical alternative to this problem. By measuring BMI gain when children are not in school, we develop an estimate of "what would have happened" had they not gone to school at all. The summer provides an opportunity to observe the nonschool effect, which, when compared with the school-year results, provides an estimate of the difference between school and nonschool conditions.

Analyzing a national sample of over seventeen thousand chil-dren from the Early Childhood Longitudinal Study (ECLS-K) data during their kindergarten and first grade school years and the summer in between, von Hippel et al. compared how quickly chil-dren gain BMI when school is in session versus when it is not.[22] One might expect a modest increase in BMI gain from the kinder-garten year to the summer after for maturation reasons, but the authors observed BMI gain during the summer that was roughly three times the kindergarten rate, a much greater increase than normal maturation would predict. Even more telling was that BMI gain during the first grade year was *less* (about half) than that observed during the previous summer.[23] And whereas most chil-dren experienced better health outcomes during the school year than during summer, this was especially true for black and His-panic children and for children who were already obese at the start of kindergarten. These results direct our attention to nonschool environments, especially for children most at risk for obesity, as the primary source of BMI gain.

---

## *Conclusion*

Traditional research methods have told us little about whether being in school is better or worse for children's health. Seasonal comparison work suggests that, at least on average, children experience healthier BMI gain when in school versus not. This is an important finding because it helps direct efforts to reduce childhood obesity. Had we found results showing that BMI gains are fastest when children are in school, we would have turned our attention to school reforms. But the fact that BMI gains are fastest when school is out directs our attention toward children's nonschool environments as the main source of the problem. Schools appear to reduce the BMI gain most children would otherwise have experienced.

Unfortunately, because of limitations in the data, von Hippel et al. were not able to determine exactly why rates of BMI growth are greater during summer vacations than during the school year. Part of the explanation may be related to the finding that being a racial or ethnic minority is associated with a faster BMI growth rate during the summer, although rates of growth are similar across racial-ethnic categories during the school year. Compared with white students, minority children are exposed to more fast-food restaurants and convenience foods, more television, and neighborhood conditions that are not conducive to outside physical activity.[24] For these children, the school structure may provide healthier foods and more opportunity for physical exercise than their home environments and communities. Of course, this might explain some of the racial-ethnic patterns but does little to account for why the summer vacation environment is less healthy, on average, for all students.

Schools may be better for the average student because, despite some faults, they offer structure by limiting the amount of food intake time available and usually provide the opportunity for at least some physical activity. In contrast, while children are at home, they may have greater access to snacks throughout the day. Furthermore, although the summer months generally offer better weather, children may spend this time in activities that burn few calories (watching television and playing video games). The summer months also offer the opportunity for children to experience less supervised time. As one example, parents may not enforce regular bed times as consistently, and irregular sleep patterns, which have been associated with greater risk for obesity in adults,[25] may also contribute to childhood BMI gains.

Concluding that school environments are healthier than nonschool environments for most children may strike some as odd, given that schools are notorious for poor-quality lunches. But because the quality of children's nonschool environments is so variable and the variation in school quality less variable (recall Figure 2.1), children end up exhibiting more similar, and healthier, outcomes during the school year than during summer. This is not to say that schools are serving nutritious lunches or that they could not do more to improve their children's health but rather that nonschool environments appear to be the larger culprit.

The main source of BMI growth appears to be nonschool factors, but this still tells us little about why children's obesity has tripled from 5 to 15 percent in the past two decades.[26] Has something changed in children's out-of-school lives that would result in such a dramatic increase? Resolving this problem will not be easy given that the nonschool environment is less amenable than the school environment to policy manipulation. Implementing school policies as a way of improving children's health is not without merit—schools could do better than they currently do—but we anticipate that the most successful school policies will be those that influence children's lives outside of school, where they spend the vast majority of their time. Some of these programs deliberately involve parents in the process of learning about nutrition and exercise and so hold the promise of influencing the nonschool environment.[27] Finally, because children exhibit healthier BMI gains when in school versus not, increasing the number of days children are in school would play a positive role in reducing childhood obesity. When thinking of childhood obesity as a "public issue," the more school, the better.

## Notes

1. Ogden, C. L., Flegal, K. M., Carroll, M. D., & Johnson, C. L. (2002). Prevalence and trends in overweight among U.S. children and adolescents. *Journal of the American Medical Association, 288*, 1728–1732.

2. Mills, C. W. (1959). *The sociological imagination.* New York: Oxford University Press.

3. U.S. Department of Education, National Center for Education Statistics. (2005). *Digest of education statistics, 2004* (NCES No. 2006-005). Chap 1. Retrieved September 5, 2006, from http://nces.ed.gov/programs/digest/d04/ch_1.asp; *Projections of education statistics to 2014* (NCES No. 2005-074). Section 1. Retrieved September 5, 2006, from http://nces.ed.gov/programs/projections/sec_1a.asp.

4. Carter, R. C. (2002). The impact of public schools on childhood obesity. *Journal of the American Medical Association, 288*, 2180. Sallis, J. F., Conway, T. L., Prochaska, J. J., McKenzie, T. L., Marshall, S. J., & Brown, M. (2001). The association of school environments with youth physical activity. *American Journal of Public Health, 91*, 618–620.

5. Associated Press. (2006, June 4). Obesity letters having effect in Arkansas. *New York Times.*

6. Fleming-Moran, M., & Thiagarajah, K. (2005). Behavioral interventions and the role of television in the growing epidemic of adolescent obesity: Data from the 2001 Youth Risk Behavioral Survey. *Methods of Information in Medicine, 44*, 303–309; Kaur, H., Choi, W. S., Mayo, M. S., & Harris, K. J. (2003). Duration of television watching is associated with increased body mass index. *Journal of Pediatrics, 143*, 506–511; Robinson, T. N. (2001). Television viewing and childhood obesity. *Pediatric Clinics of North America, 48*, 1017–1025.

7. Walberg, H. J. (1984). Families as partners in educational productivity. *Phi Delta Kappan, 65*, 397–400.

8. Chen, E., Matthews, K. A., & Boyce, W. T. (2002). Socioeconomic differences in children's health: How and why do these relationships change with age? *Psychological Bulletin, 128*, 295–329; Wright, R. J., Mitchell, H., Visness, C. M., Cohen, S., Stout, J., Evans, R., et al. (2004). Community violence and asthma morbidity: The Inner-City Asthma Study. *American Journal of Public Health, 94*, 625–632.

9. Chen et al. (2002); Klinnert, M. D., Nelson, H. S., Price, M. R., Adinoff, A. D., Leung, D.Y.M., & Mrazek, D. A. (2001). Onset and persistence of childhood asthma: Predictors from infancy. *Pediatrics, 108*, E69; McLeod, J. D., & Shanahan, M. J. (1996). Trajectories of poverty and children's mental health. *Journal of Health and Social Behavior, 37*, 207–220.

10. Heyns, B. (1978). *Summer learning and the effects of schooling.* New York: Academic Press.

11. Seasonal comparisons are most effective under conditions where there is arguably little spillover between seasons—that is, that school characteristics do not have important influences on subsequent summer learning. If summer learning depends in an important way on school practices from the previous year, then it fails to provide an uncontaminated measure of learning due to nonschool factors. Because there are so few seasonal data available, the spillover assumption is difficult to evaluate with confidence, but the current empirical information suggests that the assumption of minimal spillover is reasonable (for a more detailed discussion, see Downey, D. B., von Hippel, P. T., & Hughes, M. [2005]. Paper presented at the American Sociological Association meetings in Philadelphia on August 13–16, 2005.

12. The research design is comparable to one sometimes employed in health research where patients are observed while exposed to a particular treatment and then again while off the treatment.

13. Heyns. (1978); Entwisle, D. R., & Alexander, K. L. (1992). Summer setback: Race, poverty, school composition, and math achievement in the first two years of school. *American Sociological Review, 57,* 72–84; Entwisle, D. R., & Alexander, K. L. (1994). The gender gap in math: Its possible origins in neighborhood effects. *American Sociological Review, 59,* 822–838; Downey, D. B., von Hippel, P. T., & Broh, B. (2004). Are schools the great equalizer? Using seasonal comparisons to assess schooling's role in inequality. *American Sociological Review, 69,* 613–635.

14. Entwisle & Alexander. (1992).

15. Heyns. (1978).

16. Entwisle & Alexander. (1992); Entwisle & Alexander. (1994).

17. Downey, von Hippel, & Broh. (2004).

18. Bowles, S., & Gintis, H. (1976). *Schooling in capitalist America: Educational reform and the contradictions of economic life.* New York: Basic Books; Bourdieu, P. (1977). *Reproduction in education, society, and culture.* Beverly Hills, CA: Sage; Collins, R. (1979). *The credential society: An historical sociology of education and stratification.* New York: Academic Press.

19. Condron, D. J., & Roscigno, V. J. (2003). Disparities within: Unequal spending and achievement in an urban school district. *Sociology of Education, 76,* 18–36.

20. Downey, von Hippel, & Hughes. (2005).

21. Downey, von Hippel, & Hughes. (2005).

22. Von Hippel, P. T., Powell, B., Downey, D. B., & Rowland, N. J. (2007). Changes to children's body mass index (BMI) during the school year and during summer vacation. *American Journal of Public Health, 97*(4), 696–702.

23. In addition, a smaller group of initially underweight children also exhibited healthier patterns of growth and greater BMI gain for them during the school year versus during the summer.

24. Kumanyika, S., & Grier, S. (2006). Targeting interventions for ethnic minority and low-income populations. *Future of Children, 16,* 187–207; Morland K., Wing, S., Diez Roux, A., & Poole, C. (2002). Neighborhood characteristics associated with the location of food stores and food service places.

*American Journal of Preventative Medicine, 22*, 23–29; Powell, K. E., Martin, L. M., & Chowdhury, P. P. (2003). Places to walk: Convenience and regular physical activity. *American Journal of Public Health, 93*, 1519–1521.

25. Gangswisch, J. E., Malaspina, D., Boden-Albala, B., & Heymsfield, S. B. (2005). Inadequate sleep as a risk factor for obesity: Analyses of the NHANES I. *Sleep, 28*, 1289–1296.

26. Ogden et al. (2002).

27. Lindsay, A. C., Sussner, K. M., Kim, J., & Gortmaker, S. (2006). The role of parents in preventing childhood obesity. *Future of Children, 16*, 169–186.

DOUGLAS B. DOWNEY *is a professor of sociology at Ohio State University.*

HEATHER R. BOUGHTON *is a doctoral student at Ohio State University.*

*A successful summer learning program approaches learning intentionally and develops the program's infrastructure components.*

# 3

# Characteristics of effective summer learning programs in practice

*Susanne R. Bell, Natalie Carrillo*

IN 2005, RESEARCHERS AND STAFF at the Center for Summer Learning at Johns Hopkins University examined various summer program models and the evidence of their effectiveness. As a result of this research, the center published a handbook describing the characteristics of effective summer learning programs. The nine characteristics provide a framework for profiles contained in this chapter and demonstrate how effective practices lead to positive results for young people. Research demonstrates that programs that employ the attributes described by these characteristics demonstrate success in two areas for their attendees: accelerating academic performance and supporting positive youth development.[1] For young people to have maximum benefit, a program must endeavor to implement all of the characteristics.

The nine characteristics of effective summer learning programs divide into two sections. The first three characteristics address a program's approach to learning:

NEW DIRECTIONS FOR YOUTH DEVELOPMENT, NO. 114, SUMMER 2007 © WILEY PERIODICALS, INC.
Published online in Wiley InterScience (www.interscience.wiley.com) • DOI: 10.1002/yd.212

1. Intentional focus on accelerating learning
2. Firm commitment to youth development
3. Proactive approach to summer learning

These attributes address the program's intent to support holistic child development. The second section covers the crucial role of program infrastructure to ensuring the organization achieves and maintains quality programming. The last six characteristics are

4. Strong, empowering leadership
5. Advanced, collaborative planning
6. Extensive opportunities for staff development
7. Strategic partnerships
8. Rigorous approach to evaluation and commitment to program improvement
9. Clear focus on sustainability and cost-effectiveness.[2]

An effective program speeds up learning rather than allowing students' knowledge to slip away over the summer and employs positive youth development practices.

## *Approach to learning*

Although there often appears to be a division between the education and youth development fields, logic and research indicate the two practices are integrally linked. The approach-to-learning characteristics take a holistic view of young people's development. Programs that take this approach reflect positive outcomes: higher school-year attendance and achievement, increased motivation to learn, increased feelings of belonging, and reduced participation in risky behavior. For programs to accelerate learning effectively, instruction should not merely replicate traditional school-year content or methods. Rather, summer instructional techniques are most effective when academic learning is woven into enrichment activities like field trips or learning a new skill. These opportunities for

NEW DIRECTIONS FOR YOUTH DEVELOPMENT • DOI: 10.1002/yd

enhancing young people's knowledge should complement school-year teaching in content so that children return to school in the fall.

Youth development generally refers to an approach or process by which adults, organizations, and communities provide opportunities and supports so that young people can achieve and demonstrate a set of desired outcomes.[3] Meaningful relationships that make the difference in the life of a young person are at the core of youth development beliefs. For young people to create and maintain relationships with peers and caring adults, interactions should be planned intentionally.

Both an intent on accelerating learning and a commitment to youth development lead to the most important task of summer programs: preventing summer learning loss and narrowing the expansion of the achievement gap.

## Program infrastructure

The second set of characteristics expresses the theory behind the infrastructural components that make up the fourth through ninth characteristics of effective summer learning programs. The roles, tasks, and decisions of the program's leadership determine everything else that will follow. Outstanding programs tap into empowering leadership techniques so that staff members at all levels are supported in their tasks. This would include staff access to tools, resources, and information. Most important, staff would feel confident in their ability to tackle problems and take responsibility for their actions.

Program leaders play a key role in facilitating an advanced, collaborative program-planning process that offers stakeholders a voice. Not only are program staff stakeholders, but so are community members, customers, and partners. All of these audiences buy into the plan to fulfill their responsibilities to the organization and their students. Ideally, planning would begin at least six months in advance of the program's start date. Even the most experienced program must allot planning time to produce high-quality learning and engagement opportunities for young people. But beyond yearly planning, an excellent program will undertake a strategic planning process.

Staff development can be a challenge for summer programs because of the combination of year-round and seasonal staff. The varied backgrounds of employees can also present a challenge. For staff development to be useful, it must be relevant. In the following profiles, programs have addressed this need in multiple ways. The solutions to staff development are as unique as the programs.

Before considering the components of a healthy strategic partnership, we need to address what constitutes a strategic partnership. A strategic partnership is mutually beneficial, adds value to all partners, and meets a critical need. All partners understand what they hope to gain and what their partners hope to gain from the relationship. The mission and vision of each organization should be enhanced by the partnership. An offshoot of partnership relationships are relationships with stakeholders, people who are needed to maintain program support and interest.

Evaluation is a continual process. Programs committed to rigorous evaluation and program improvement collect feedback, measure progress, report outcomes, and work to improve the quality of their services.[4] The first step in evaluation is defining performance indicators, which should encompass both academic and youth development goals. Measurement techniques such as surveys, academic assessment, and observation should be considered when creating performance indicators. Most important, the data collected should be used to improve program practices and should be shared with all stakeholders in a timely manner to facilitate buy-in and organizational transparency.

Finally, and often most challenging, effective summer programs plan for sustainability and cost-effectiveness. Sustainability is the ability to meet the current needs of the organization and program while actively preparing for future needs.[5] Although program leadership usually manages this task, staff members must each be aware of and responsive to the program's vision, mission, and strategies that support sustainability. For maximum effectiveness, strategic planning and sustainability efforts should interrelate, align with the organization's mission, and be clearly communicated to all stakeholders. Cost-effectiveness, the relationship between financial costs and program results, is an important component of sustainability. Understanding cost-effectiveness is beneficial because it allows programs to clearly articulate outcomes. This clear communication is useful for funder, partner, and stakeholder relationships.

## Program profiles

The following profiles are of thirteen programs that were applicants to the Center for Summer Learning's Excellence in Summer Learning Award. This award recognizes outstanding summer programs that demonstrate excellence in accelerating academic achievement and promoting positive development for young people between kindergarten and twelfth grade. Given annually, the goal of the Excellence in Summer Learning Award is to identify and highlight programs providing high-quality summer learning experiences for youth. Both the application procedure and the review process were based on the characteristics described earlier.

In 2006, the reviewers promoted thirteen programs into the second round: Building Educated Leaders for Life (BELL); CentroNía; Covenant House Washington; Discovery Creek; Family Technology Resource Center; Harlem Educational Activities Fund, Inc.; Harlem RBI; Higher Achievement Program; Milwaukee Public Schools; Newport Partnership for Families; Parks & People Foundation; Summerbridge Pittsburgh; and Trail Blazers. These programs apply a range of techniques to support young people's development and accelerate learning such as rigorous academic instruction, exploration of the natural world, and enrichment opportunities.

Each of the thirteen programs participated in an interview with reviewers who inquired about a typical program day, how the program used its evaluation data, and the program's greatest achievement. Based on this interview and the application, the center honored a record four programs with the Excellence in Summer Learning Award in 2006: BELL, Harlem RBI, Higher Achievement Program, and Trail Blazers.

NEW DIRECTIONS FOR YOUTH DEVELOPMENT • DOI: 10.1002/yd

The variety of instructional and organizational practices described in the profiles illustrates the range of possibilities that compose an excellent summer learning program. There is not a single prescribed model to creating an outstanding program where young people are supported in their growth over the summer months. Rather, what is most interesting about this collection of programs is their shared commitment to quality programming and to meeting the needs of young people, families, and their communities during the critical summer months.

- Organization: BELL
- Program name: BELL Accelerated Learning Summer Program
- Date of initial operation: 1996
- Number of youth served annually through summer program: 3,750
- Student-to-staff ratio: 1:8
- Highlighted characteristic: Rigorous approach to evaluation and commitment to program improvement

The mission of BELL is to increase the educational achievements, self-esteem, and life opportunities of elementary school children living in low-income urban communities. In 1996, to counter the summer learning losses of participants, BELL began its Accelerated Learning Summer Program (BELL Summer).

BELL maintains a rigorous approach to evaluation and a commitment to program improvement. BELL Summer has four major goals for participants: improve academic performance; enhance self-concept and attitude toward learning; develop social skills, leadership abilities, and a perception of themselves as contributing members of a community; and engage their parents as educational facilitators and advocates. For over six years, BELL has been engaged in formal outcome measurement. Preprogram and postprogram assessments of academic skills are used to objectively measure improvement. BELL Summer teachers complete progress reports midway and at the conclusion of the program. Parent and staff perspective on goal achievement is collected through postprogram surveys and focus groups. BELL's evaluation advisory board, governing board, and management team review the program outcomes every year to determine the most effective elements of their program model and areas for improvement. Data from the previous summer are used in the planning process. These data are reported in a "Lessons Learned" report issued to senior management in November before the launch of the formal project plan in December. BELL uses the data to refine elements and replicate successful elements.

In 2004, BELL scholars gained an average of six months of grade-equivalent skills in reading and math during the six-week program. Over the course of the summer, these participants moved closer to their peers nationally, performing at the fiftieth and forty-second percentiles in reading and math, respectively, by the end of the program compared with the forty-third and thirty-first percentiles when the program began.

During the summers of 2004 and 2005, BELL participated in an independent third-party evaluation to measure the extent to which BELL Summer contributes to the learning gains of children in low-income communities compared with students who did not participate. This study used an experimental design and offers the field the first experimental evidence of a multisite summer program. The independent study yielded a statistically positive effect on students' reading skills and parents' home reading habits in comparison to the control group.

- Organization: CentroNía
- Program name: CentroNía School Age/Youth Development Summer Program
- Location: Washington, DC
- Date of initial operation: 1986
- Number of youth served annually: about 200
- Student-to-staff ratio: 1:10
- Highlighted characteristic: Strategic partnerships

CentroNía provides comprehensive education and family support services to nearly a thousand low-income predominantly African American and Latino and African immigrant individuals.

The program provides holistic support to children, youth, and their families, incorporating an outcomes-based curriculum with a multi-cultural foundation and arts-integrated pedagogy. Integrating the arts with other subject areas combines the hands-on creativity of the arts (visual, performing, and literary) with the focused content of subjects such as math, science, language arts, and social studies.

CentroNía developed an integral web of strategic partnerships with local arts institutions, including the Corcoran Museum, the Levine School of Music, The Freer Art Gallery, and the District of Columbia Public Access Television. All of these organizations participate by offering classes for participants, organizing trips, and providing vital staff professional development. In addition, CentroNía's Multidisciplinary Arts Program uses its relationships to accelerate learning opportunities for students who want to continue rigorous arts instruction. CentroNía's arts program has secured student scholarships at institutions such as the Corcoran College of Art and Design, Young Playwrights Theater, DC Dance Theater, GALA Hispanic Theater, and other organizations. Through its many affiliations, CentroNía's students have received innumerable opportunities to attend art exhibits and other events.

The program engages youth participants in language acquisition, multidisciplinary arts activities, literacy, recreation, technology, and youth leadership. The goal is that students will acquire a basic knowledge and vocabulary to articulate their ideas and visions in addition to supplementing the foundation of their traditional academic settings.

- Organization: Covenant House Washington, Prevention Services
- Program name: Summer Enrichment Program
- Date of initial operation: 1999
- Number of youth served annually through summer program: 150
- Student-to-staff ratio: 8–10:1
- Highlighted characteristic: A firm commitment to youth development

The Summer Enrichment Program (SEP) is designed to meet the needs of youth aged eleven to seventeen at high risk for teen pregnancy, substance abuse, violence, and low educational attainment. The program enhances young people's academic skills while expanding their life experiences through community service projects, recreation, and cultural outings. Developing participants' social and familial relationships is also a goal of the summer program.

The academic portion of the program occurs in the morning during the seven- to eight-week summer program. The students attend math, language arts, social studies, and technology classes that focus on cultural or youth-centered themes. Participants experience cultural and recreational enrichment through field trips and activities. Guest speakers visit the program and engage youth in group discussions on topics such as politics and substance abuse.

Following the morning academic component, youth select from a range of activities such as community service opportunities or arts projects. The students can participate in the Youth Advisory Board, which helps members to develop leadership skills and self-awareness while providing a service to their community. Youth can also expand their abilities in the Peer Leadership Training program, which provides peer mentoring, career exploration opportunities, and job-readiness skill development. Both the Youth Advisory Board and Peer Leadership Training allow youth to develop skills to ensure their future success while providing feedback to the program.

- Organization: Discovery Creek Children's Museum of Washington
- Program name: Summer Nature Adventure Programs
- Date of initial operation: 1996
- Number of youth served annually through summer program: 1,400 in 2006
- Student-to-staff ratio: 6:1
- Highlighted characteristic: Proactive approach to summer learning

Discovery Creek Children's Museum of Washington provides meaningful outdoor experiences that are hands-on and minds-on to Washington, D.C.'s underserved children. The museum's staff members are committed to helping children experience, appreciate, and become stewards of the natural environment by educating through ecoimmersion exhibitions, live animal demonstrations, and dynamic interactive teaching.

Planning for the Summer Nature Adventure Programs is a year-round process. The summer program managers create a work plan with a highly organized breakdown of monthly tasks. This work plan is constantly updated and revised to reflect the most efficient operational practices and procedures. The summer program staff schedule time throughout the year to meet with all staff members. Meeting topics include professional development opportunities and discussions in behavior management, program content, and strategies for working with children. Discovery Creek ensures that all full-time staff members are trained in educational approaches that include experiential education, object-based learning, inquiry-based learning, place-based education, and immersion education.

Each summer session is designed around a theme and teaches environmental education through science, art, culture, history, play, team building, and outdoor adventure. Each day is planned by staff members to include a variety of activities that engage the mind of every child. The goal at Discovery Creek is to find a way to connect with every child and spark that child's interest in science or the natural world.

- Organization: Family Technology Resource Center
- Program name: Summer Extravaganza
- Date of initial operation: 2001
- Number of youth served annually through summer program: 460
- Student-to-staff ratio: 3:1
- Highlighted characteristic: Extensive opportunities for staff development

Summer Extravaganza is one of many programs offered through the Family Technology Resource Center (FTRC) and was created five years ago in response to teacher requests to reform science, math, and technology education for children. Educators were concerned that children were losing their intrinsic interest in science and that young girls were beginning to believe the adage that girls are not good at science or math.

Summer Extravaganza is a project-based science, math, and technology program where each summer teams explore real-world issues. The program provides students an opportunity to learn from and with teachers, scientists, college students, and professors on a university campus. It also provides teachers with materials they can integrate into their regular classrooms.

Professional development is critical to program success. Yearly, the Center for Education Integrating Science, Math, and Computing and the Georgia Tech Research Institute conduct a fifty-hour course to prepare teachers for the upcoming Summer Extravaganza. Educators earn credit for their teaching recertification from the course. Through professional development opportunities, teachers, paraprofessionals, and other partners learn effective instructional strategies. Summer Extravaganza believes that as many teachers as possible should participate so educators can incorporate science, math, and technology into classroom instruction. The program hopes increased effective integration of technology into the curriculum will boost female and minority enrollment in higher education over the long term.

- Organization: Harlem Educational Activities Fund, Inc.
- Program name: Summer Quest
- Date of initial operation: 1999
- Number of youth served annually through summer program: 125 in 2005
- Student-to-staff ratio: 12:1
- Highlighted characteristic: Firm commitment to youth development

Harlem Educational Activities Fund, Inc. (HEAF), is an education and youth development organization that works to help motivated students develop the intellectual curiosity, academic ability, social values, and personal resilience they need to ensure success in school, career, and life. Students are identified in middle school and supported through a variety of out-of-school-time academic and youth development programs through college.

HEAF's Summer Quest Program provides summer enrichment opportunities to students who do not typically participate in quality academic summer programs. Summer Quest's dynamic model builds academic skill and engages minds through fun and exciting activities. Students' interests drive the content of project-based classes, which are designed to foster collaboration, communication, and leadership skills. Summer Quest activities range from academic classes to test preparation for the New York City Specialized High School Admissions Test. Recent electives included Project Restaurant, AI: Build a Bot, CSI Harlem, Order in the Court, Comic Creations, and the Fantastic Four: Elements of Hip Hop. The asset-rich environment promotes character development and social skills. HEAF's young scholars explore issues of ethics, values, leadership, and identity through Summer Quest activities. As students meet these challenges, they increase their self-confidence and broaden their self-concept.

- Organization: Harlem RBI
- Program name: Reading and Enrichment Academy for Learning (REAL) Kids
- Date of initial operation: 1999
- Number of youth served annually through summer program: 240 in 2006, 270 in 2007
- Student-to-staff ratio: 5:1
- Highlighted characteristic: Proactive approach to summer learning

Harlem RBI is a community-based youth development organization that uses baseball, softball, and the power of teams to provide inner-city youth with opportunities to play, learn, and grow, inspiring them to recognize their potential and realize their dreams. The goal of the REAL Kids Program is to provide structured academic, enrichment, and sports programming in a supportive and engaging environment. Specific goals include the prevention of summer learning loss, an increase in literacy skills, the fostering of positive social skills, and the improvement of physical fitness and health for all participants.

The objectives are achieved through several proactive strategies. Whether in the classroom, on the ball field, or on a field trip, participants' developmental needs are met as they come to value and enjoy learning, cultivate their physical abilities, and build meaningful relationships. The program has five main components: literacy workshops, team clubhouse, baseball or softball teams, field trips, and a sleep-away camp.

Coaches may lead a discussion about the team's experiences on the field in which they discuss conflict and celebrate success. The youth receive writing challenges such as composing a cheer or poem. Problem-solving initiatives are offered daily through conflict resolution role-plays and reflective discussions. Last, youth create a summer-long project using listening, speaking, reading, and writing skills, which are the four elements of literacy. Past projects have included a video documentary, a sports highlight show, and life-sized baseball cards. Harlem RBI has created a proactive learning experience while giving young people the opportunity to have fun, enjoy new experiences, and develop friendships.

- Organization: Higher Achievement Program
- Program name: Higher Achievement Summer Academy
- Date of initial operation: 1975
- Number of youth served annually through summer program: 460
- Student-to-staff ratio: 12:1
- Highlighted characteristic: Intentional focus on accelerating learning

Higher Achievement is a year-round high school preparatory program for disadvantaged middle-school children. Higher Achievement's mission is to develop academic habits and behaviors in vulnerable middle-school children to increase their educational opportunities. The organization's goals are to improve student academic achievement, to send all program graduates to top high schools, and to make academic excellence a valued goal in all communities. The program combines advanced social justice-oriented curricula, with individual mentoring and high school placement. Higher Achievement fills service gaps with a four-year sustained academic intervention during the most critical years in a child's social and academic development. This intervention builds students' skills and attitudes that affect achievement and works to continue this progress through to college acceptance.

Over each summer of their middle-school years, participants attend classes that follow an accelerated version of local standards for learning and develop basic academic skills like note taking and managing a planner. Scholars participate in weekly field trips and a three-day university trip to experience college life. The Summer Academy bolsters scholars' academic skills, self-confidence, and critical thinking skills.

In many urban public school systems, a lack of academic opportunity results in underachievement. Higher Achievement reverses this cycle with opportunities like relationships with mentors, accelerated and hands-on academic work, and top school placement that develop and reward academic progress. These chances for growth encourage student interest, which increases student effort, which in turn leads to academic achievement and ultimately to the opportunity to attend a top high school.

The curriculum combines skill acquisition with experiential learning activities and academic skill building. Whether simulating a United Nations debate or measuring the amount of carbon dioxide in a running tail pipe, scholars are introduced to advanced concepts through methods that inspire their curiosity and increase their confidence.

- Organization: Milwaukee Public Schools
- Program name: Summer Community Learning Centers (CLCs) Program
- Date of initial operation: 1999
- Number of youth served annually through summer program: 5,248 (summer school); 5,971 (CLCs)
- Student-to-staff ratio: 15–20:1 (summer school); 20:1 (CLCs)
- Highlighted characteristic: Strategic partnerships

NEW DIRECTIONS FOR YOUTH DEVELOPMENT · DOI: 10.1002/yd

Milwaukee Public Schools (MPS) is a large urban decentralized school district serving over 93,500 students. One of the district's six core beliefs is that community partnerships add value. This belief is upheld through a myriad of district initiatives, including the Summer CLC program, which has established a large number of partnerships to provide summer programming to some of Milwaukee's neediest youth, 87 percent of whom qualified for free or reduced-fee school lunch.

Youth enrolled in the Summer CLC Program, held at over thirty middle and elementary schools, receive wrap-around services that include academic support, nutritious meals, and exposure to enriching activities and caring adults, all of which support student learning and health.

The success of Milwaukee's Summer CLC Program is due to the collaborative efforts of the MPS Division of Community Recreation, MPS Facilities and Maintenance Services, MPS School Nutrition Services, MPS Summer School Office, and ten Milwaukee-area community-based organizations. Additional partnerships are established through the Summer School planning committee, which comprises district employees from curriculum and instruction, school nutrition, transportation, recreation, bilingual and special education, guidance, school safety, and certified or classified staffing.

The CLC program also works in partnership with its community partners to seek funding for this valuable program. Moreover, Milwaukee's CLCs are highly represented on the Wisconsin Afterschool Network, which advocates for state-level funding appropriations.

- Organization: Newport Partnership for Families
- Program name: Reading Reaps Rewards
- Date of initial operation: 2001
- Number of youth served annually through summer program: 250 in 2004, 400 in 2005
- Student-to-staff ratio: 13:1
- Highlighted characteristic: Advanced, collaborative planning

The Newport Partnership for Families works to develop and maintain an integrated network of services that are responsive to the needs of all families, are culturally sensitive, and focus on the strengths of each family. The partnership is committed to developing high-quality programs that foster self-sufficiency, high educational standards, and true parental involvement. The partnership joined Newport, Rhode Island, Public Schools; Newport Public Education; and local community agencies to design a comprehensive summer literacy plan. This model brings all of the services and opportunities together to offer students the literacy opportunities they need within summer recreational programs.

The partnership's educational success committee oversees all aspects of the Reading Reaps Rewards (R3) program. The committee meets monthly ten months a year. In the fall, the committee processes information from the previous year, including evaluation results. These sessions focus on what worked and what needs to be changed to overcome barriers to success. Winter meetings focus on the next year's program, primarily defining and securing the needed resources. This process results in a strategic plan that gains broad support from program participants, members, and funders.

By design, and in all implementation aspects, the summer reading program is a collaborative process, with its agenda and decision driven by partners. The vision is held by all members of the partnership community, including parents.

- Organization: Parks & People Foundation
- Program name: SuperKids Camp
- Date of initial operation: 1997
- Number of youth served annually through summer program: 1,000
- Student-to-staff ratio: 1:10
- Highlighted characteristic: Rigorous approach to evaluation and commitment to program improvement

The Parks & People Foundation's SuperKids Camp (SKC) program is dedicated to the prevention of summer learning loss and to early childhood literacy development. The goals of the camp are building reading skills, creating and implementing a replicable model for effective community partnerships, and assisting in the recruitment of new teachers to the Baltimore City Public School System.

To meet their goals, SKC conducts various forms of evaluation of the students' reading levels and their program. They conduct a before-and-after standardized vocabulary and comprehension test. Each site administrator provides weekly reports on the number of lessons mastered and the number of books read by each child. An in-depth evaluation is also completed by a qualified outside evaluator.

The research design includes both quantitative and qualitative data collection. The Dynamic Indicators of Basic Early Literacy Skills, sixth edition (DIBELS), test indicates whether students have the requisite literacy skills necessary for grade promotion. The second data source is a modified version of the Garfield Reading Survey, which measures student reading motivation and camp-related experiences. Finally, a staff survey captures staff perceptions of the curriculum, student performance, and parental involvement. Daily attendance is also an important data source. Program reports from SKC enrichment providers are also reviewed to determine the degree to which they met objectives.

Data sources revealed a clear and positive impact of SKC on students' ability to read. On all measures of the DIBELS, students demonstrated statistically significant growth. The Garfield Student Survey revealed that students' motivation to read was strong at the conclusion of camp and that students thoroughly enjoyed many elements of the curriculum. Staff surveys indicated an overwhelming improvement in reading ability, reading interest, and attitude toward reading by students. Further, by the end of the six-week camp, students were prepared for the next grade.

- Organization: Summerbridge Pittsburgh
- Program name: Summerbridge Pittsburgh Summer Program
- Date of initial operation: 1994
- Number of youth served annually through summer program: 150
- Student-to-staff ratio: 4:1
- Highlighted characteristic: Clear focus on sustainability and cost-effectiveness

Summerbridge Pittsburgh (SBP) provides a tuition-free, two-year, life-changing experience that empowers at-risk middle-school students to achieve academic success and inspires young adults to pursue careers in education. By using a high-energy approach to learning and leadership, middle-school students gain the academic and leadership skills critical to future educational success, and high school and college-age teachers learn that the best educators are driven by dedication and passion. SBP is a six-week intensive summer session that students attend for two consecutive summers. They use the "student-teaching-students" model of educational empowerment.

SBP has an expansive network of diverse partners, including corporations, foundations, cultural institutions, public and independent schools, colleges and universities, and SBP families. The support of Sewickley Academy, SBP's educational partner, is critical to sustaining the work of SBP. The Sewickley Academy's business office coordinates with the SBP director to oversee and maintain all financial issues. The academy's development director supports SBP in soliciting and securing funding from diverse entities and seeking an appropriate balance among foundation, corporation, and individual support. Because of the strength of SBP's relationship with the academy, the strong program infrastructure in place, and a significant endowment fund, SBP could sustain its work should the support of a major funder be lost.

- Organization: Trail Blazers
- Program name: Trail Blazers Summer Program
- Date of initial operation: 1887
- Number of youth served annually through summer program: 350
- Student-to-staff ratio: 1:3
- Highlighted characteristic: Strong, empowering leadership

Trail Blazers facilitates the development of values and life skills essential for productive citizenship in inner-city youth. The summer program helps children develop a love of learning; build interpersonal skills; and increase self-confidence, self-esteem, and self-reliance. The Trail Blazers program provides educational opportunity for at-risk youth.

Trail Blazers forges lasting and effective relationships between group leaders and the children and works with each camper for a minimum of three years. Children are introduced to Trail Blazers through the Summer Program and then participate in year-round programming including the education weekends, mentoring, and leadership training. The Summer Program has two goals: to develop a love of learning and an increase in the time spent reading and writing and to enhance interpersonal skills and the ability to interact appropriately with peers and adults.

The structure of the camp was also established to provide leadership for the children. The executive director lives on site during the summer months to manage all operations. Each camp director supervises a team of three "enablers," who are at least nineteen years old and must be enrolled or have graduated from a college or university. Many group leaders are former campers. They also employ an education coordinator, a certified teacher who oversees education efforts and works with two literacy coordinators to implement academic programming.

### Notes

1. Fairchild, R., McLaughlin, B., & Brady, J. (2006). *Making the most of summer: A handbook on effective summer programming and thematic learning*. Baltimore: Center for Summer Learning.
2. Fairchild, McLaughlin, & Brady. (2006).
3. Fairchild, McLaughlin, & Brady. (2006).
4. Morley, E., Vinson, E., & Hatry, H. (2001). *A look at outcome measurement in non-profit agencies*. Washington, DC: Nonprofit Sector Research Fund.
5. Fairchild, McLaughlin, & Brady. (2006).

SUSANNE R. BELL *is a senior research program coordinator at the Center for Summer Learning at the Johns Hopkins University School of Education.*

NATALIE CARRILLO *is a research assistant at the Center for Summer Learning working toward a master's degree in public policy from the Institute for Policy Studies at Johns Hopkins University.*

*Summer programming in poor rural communities*
*requires the development of community resources,*
*human capital, and program accessibility.*

# 4

# Summer programming in rural communities: Unique challenges

*Ruthellen Phillips, Stacey Harper,*
*Susan Gamble*

WE HAVE AN IDYLLIC VIEW of summer in rural communities: fresh air, garden vegetables, vacation Bible school, ice-cold lemonade, and playing outdoors with friends. But for many children living in rural areas, summers are empty bellies, hours of boredom, and unsupervised care. Rural America is home to 2.5 million children living in deep poverty. Although we usually think of poor children as those living in the city, over the past several decades, child poverty rates have been higher in rural than in urban areas.[1]

---

## Need for summer programming in rural communities
We know that it is poor children who are most affected by the typical "summer slide," who lose ground nutritionally, and who have minimal opportunities for summer activities. Given the large

NEW DIRECTIONS FOR YOUTH DEVELOPMENT, NO. 114, SUMMER 2007 © WILEY PERIODICALS, INC.
Published online in Wiley InterScience (www.interscience.wiley.com) • DOI: 10.1002/yd.213

number of poor children living in rural communities, the need for summer programming in those communities is evident.

A review of thirty studies indicated that achievement test scores decline during the summer and that low-income children experience greater losses than their middle-income peers.[2] Studies also indicate that both academic programs[3] and out-of-school-time enrichment activities[4] can have positive effects on the achievement of low-income children.

Poor children suffer nutritionally during the summer. Without school breakfast and lunch, children lose ground nutritionally and return to school in the fall less healthy than they were in the spring. Poor families must provide for an additional ten meals each week for each school-aged child, but they have no additional food resources. The U.S. Department of Agriculture's Summer Food Service Program (SFSP) can help fill the gap by providing meals to children in low-income areas. However, only about one-fifth of eligible children in the United States are receiving these summer meals.[5] In rural areas, SFSPs cannot stand alone; to be effective, they must be paired with educational or recreational summer programming.

Child and youth development activities are limited, and rural youth have fewer safe places with caring adults and constructive activities.[6] Child care is almost nonexistent, and many children are left home alone, in the care of older siblings, or in caregiver roles themselves. Low-income communities have fewer playgrounds and other places for children to play. Children spend their days in sedentary activities.

## Challenges that rural communities face

Summer programming has the ability to address the issues of academic loss, nutritional loss, and the lack of safe, constructive activities. However, poor rural communities face three major challenges in implementing summer programming: community resources, human capital, and program accessibility.

NEW DIRECTIONS FOR YOUTH DEVELOPMENT • DOI: 10.1002/yd

### Community resources

It is difficult for low-income rural communities to offer summer programs. Fewer nonprofit organizations and other community resources are available in poor rural areas, and those that exist have limited budgets. Rural schools are less likely than their urban counterparts to offer extended-school-year programs. Most external funding has stringent spending requirements, and the focus is often narrow and inflexible. Funding has often been directed at individuals rather than institutions, addressing residents' immediate needs but not allowing for building infrastructure so needed in poor rural communities.[7]

### Human capital

It is difficult for low-income rural communities to build human capital. The human capital in poor, rural communities is undeveloped, and it is difficult to attract and retain people with the skills, knowledge, and connections required to create needed institutions and build future human capital. Residents with college educations leave for better employment opportunities, creating a brain drain.[8] The existing human resources become strained as responsibilities are assumed by a small number of residents. There are limited opportunities for youth and adults to be involved in community service and to build leadership skills needed by the community.

### Program accessibility

It is difficult for rural parents to transport their children to summer programs. Sixty-eight percent of rural residents live in communities with no or limited public transportation, and many low-income residents do not know how to drive, lack a driver's license, or lack the funds to purchase and maintain a car.[9]

Transportation costs for rural residents tend to be higher than for urban residents. Rural residents are more affected by rises in gasoline prices simply because they must travel longer distances. School consolidation has increased the distance from homes to schools. Many poor rural residents rely on small, local mom-and-pop stores for gasoline, where the costs are high.

### Energy Express: Meeting the challenges of summer programming in rural communities

Energy Express is a six-week summer program designed to pro-mote the school success of children living in more than eighty low-income rural West Virginia communities. The program seeks to maintain the nutritional status and reading achievement of poor children while providing a safe and secure environment. West Virginia University Extension Service, in partnership with other public and private entities, provides statewide leadership.

Children entering first through sixth grade attend Energy Express five days a week for three and a half hours each day. Most of the college student AmeriCorps members serve as mentors and work with small groups of eight children to create a print-rich envi-ronment. Additional AmeriCorps members serve as volunteer coor-dinators. They recruit, train, supervise, and recognize preteens, teens, and other community members who contribute in a variety of ways at each Energy Express site.

Children stay in their small groups for family-style breakfast and lunch provided under the auspices of the federally funded SFSP. Seventy percent of the children are eligible for free and reduced-priced meals. The meals help maintain growth over the summer and ensure that the children are ready to learn when they return to school in the fall. Statewide, more than thirty-two hundred children participate each summer. Daily attendance averages 82 percent for this voluntary program. Program results have been consistent over the past decade; children's reading achievement increases signifi-cantly, with an average 3.5-month gain in broad reading scores.

### Building community resources through collaboration

Energy Express has found that in poor rural communities where resources are limited, collaboration is a key to successful summer programming. No one agency or organization has the resources to support needed summer programs. During the application process for Energy Express, communities must document a collaborative of at least five agencies and organizations; usually the number is higher. Members differ from site to site and are based on the resources of a given community. Examples of local collaborative members include the extension service, school systems, community action organizations, libraries, family resource networks, faith-based organizations, parent organizations, civic organizations, and youth-serving entities. Each brings different strengths and resources to summer programming. Although collaborators have a shared vision, their individual goals and objectives, often based on funding sources, may differ. One group may be focused on increasing children's reading achievement, another on feeding hungry children, and a third on building human capital through volunteerism.

This community-based approach results in quality summer programming for children through shared ownership. Although we work diligently to build community collaborations that combine resources for greater impact, we also know that collaboration has its challenges. These challenges seem minor when compared with the benefits: a way for poor rural communities to address complex problems, an enhanced capacity for community agencies and organizations, a more efficient use of limited resources, and a foundation for sustainability.

## Building human capital through service

Energy Express builds human capital by engaging college students in service. Summer opportunities are sparse in rural communities. With many academic programs requiring community service hours or internship experiences and with college costs continuing to increase, students from rural communities are unable to return home in the summer, aggravating the brain drain that rural communities face. Energy Express enables college students of all majors and backgrounds to return to their local communities to engage in service while earning money for college. AmeriCorps, a national service program, provides summer members with a modest living allowance and a $1,000 education award that can be used to pay for college expenses or qualified student loans.

Energy Express AmeriCorps members experience a significant increase in personal efficacy. The belief in one's abilities paves the way for future involvement in the community. As one AmeriCorps member wrote, "There were some bumps in the road, but I learned to have patience and I was determined. I soon realized that I could do this, and I could do it well! I gained the confidence I needed by instilling confidence in my children, and we helped each other the entire summer bloom and discover who we are. . . . they have given me the priceless gift of faith in myself that I can do anything I set my mind to."

A symbiotic relationship develops between the children and the college students. For children who have limited exposure to adults with college education, the Energy Express AmeriCorps members serve as positive role models by giving a glimpse of future possibilities. In return, the children offer invaluable insight about the daily challenges faced by families in poverty.

The brain drain can be reversed by strengthening young people's connections with the community.[10] Energy Express cultivates strong community connections with the AmeriCorps members. It is often the relationship with the children that resonates most strongly with the AmeriCorps members. The AmeriCorps members find themselves worrying about the future of their children. They care about what will happen to the children when Energy Express ends and worry about what they will eat. When college starts again, they send letters, and during school breaks, they visit to reconnect. These emotions propel the college students to return to their communities after college and provide leadership through work and service.

Energy Express also builds human capital by involving more than four thousand volunteers from the community in summer programming. Each Energy Express site averages fifty volunteers who contribute more than nine hundred hours. From preteens to senior citizens, community members have the opportunity to share existing skills and learn new ones as they make a difference in children's lives. As volunteers contribute, they develop ownership of

NEW DIRECTIONS FOR YOUTH DEVELOPMENT • DOI: 10.1002/yd

the program and a commitment to community. They become part of the solution to a community problem by focusing on a common goal. There are a variety of opportunities for community members to actively participate in Energy Express, ranging from gathering materials for art activities to making sure every child has fifteen to twenty minutes of one-on-one reading everyday to writing down the stories of young children.

About half of Energy Express volunteers are teens and preteens, many of whom come to the program every day. Energy Express enables young people to engage in meaningful community service that helps develop an ethic of service and builds community.

Energy Express also provides some tangible benefits to youth volunteers. They are in a safe environment; they eat SFSP-sponsored family-style meals with their AmeriCorps volunteer coordinator; and they receive community service hours, which are often required for high school graduation.

## Providing transportation for program accessibility

Energy Express has learned that transportation must be provided for poor rural children to participate in summer programming on a consistent basis. Eighty percent of Energy Express sites provide some type of transportation. The local school system has lots of experience transporting children and, when Title I, 21st Century, or other school-connected funds are available, it transports Energy Express children. Sometimes there is an extended-school-year program for special needs children or another funded program, and the transportation costs are shared across programs. The cost of transportation provided by the school system tends to be high, exacerbated by large busses with high fuel costs and rules and regulations governing the pay of school personnel. As a result, a number of Energy Express sites have been forced to think creatively about providing transportation. Some have partnered with local community action agencies for Head Start busses that are idle during the summer. These vehicles tend to be smaller than typical school busses, and the agencies have different hiring requirements and wage scales from those of the board of education. Church and senior center vans have been used, and in a more metropolitan area, public transit has delivered children. At several sites, parents are reimbursed mileage for transporting their children plus a couple of neighbor children. Because youth volunteers face the same transportation issues that other rural residents face, they use the same transportation that Energy Express provides to child participants.

The challenges of transportation are ongoing: The costs continue to rise; some sites can afford for the busses to travel only main roads, so children need to get from the hollows to the pick-up spot; parents' cars break down; and there is concern about the wear and tear on agency vehicles. But despite the challenges, the commitment to providing transportation remains.

Summer programming in poor rural communities has unique challenges. But as community residents, agencies, and organizations come together on behalf of children, the challenges can be met. As community resources are built, human capital is developed, program accessibility is provided, and the power of community is recognized. As a mother of an Energy Express child said, "We all become a community in the Energy Express program."[11]

### Notes

1. Nadel, W., & Sagawa, S. (2002). *America's forgotten children: Child poverty in rural America.* Retrieved May 8, 2007, from http://eric.ed.gov/ERICDocs/data/ericdocs2/content_storage_01/0000000b/80/27/a3/d5.pdf.

2. Cooper, H., Nye, B., Charlton, K., Lindsay, J., & Greathouse, S. (1996). The effects of summer vacation on achievement test scores: A narrative and meta-analytic review. *Review of Educational Research, 66*(3), 227–268.

3. Cooper, H., Charlton, K., Valentine, J. C., & Muhlenbruck, L. (2000). Making the most of summer school: A meta-analytic and narrative review. *Monographs of the Society for Research in Child Development, Serial No. 260, 65*(1).

4. Lauer, P. A., Akiba, M., Wilkerson, S. B., Apthorp, H. A., Snow, D., & Martin-Glenn, M. (2003). *The effectiveness of out-of-school-time strategies in assisting low-achieving students in reading and mathematics.* Aurora, CO: Mid-Continent Research for Education and Learning.

5. Food Research and Action Center. (2005, October). *Obesity, food insecurity, and the federal children nutrition programs: Understanding the linkages.* Retrieved May 8, 2007, from http://www.frac.org/pdf/obesity05_paper.pdf.

6. Nadel & Sagawa. (2002).

7. Nadel & Sagawa. (2002).

8. Nadel & Sagawa. (2002).

9. Friedman, P. (2004, March). Transportation needs in rural communities. *Rural Assistance Center, 2*(1). Retrieved May 8, 2007, from http://finance-project.org/Publications/transportationneedsINRAC.htm.

10. Nadel & Sagawa. (2002).

11. Miltenberger, M. W., Phillips, R. H., Pruett, B. M., & Triplett, S. K. (2002). Small groups and mentors foster relationships during summer reading program: A qualitative analysis. *Journal of Higher Education Outreach and Engagement, 7,* 101–110.

RUTHELLEN PHILLIPS, *director of Energy Express, is an extension professor at West Virginia University.*

STACEY HARPER, *AmeriCorps program coordinator for Energy Express, is an extension assistant professor at West Virginia University.*

SUSAN GAMBLE, *AmeriCorps strengthening community coordinator for Energy Express, is an extension assistant professor at West Virginia University.*

NEW DIRECTIONS FOR YOUTH DEVELOPMENT • DOI: 10.1002/yd

*Collaboration is the new mandate, and it is incumbent on all to understand collaboration's principles and practices.*

# 5

# Collaboration: Leveraging resources and expertise

*Anne Byrne, Jane Hansberry*

THE TERM *COLLABORATION* too often is used to describe any kind of cooperative activity between and among organizations. Such overuse of the term can serve to dilute the power of true collaboration, which has been defined as "a mutually beneficial and well-defined relationship entered into by two or more organizations to achieve common goals. The relationship includes a commitment to a definition of mutual relationships and goals; a jointly developed structure and shared responsibility; mutual authority and accountability for success; and sharing of resources and rewards."[1] One can discern from this definition that collaboration is distinct from cooperation and coordination.

Having established a common understanding about collaboration, one can then look to the practices of collaboration. Primary to a discussion of collaboration practice is the question, Why do organizations collaborate? To answer this question fully, consider the perspectives of three classes of nonprofit organizational stakeholders: funding sources, clients, and potential partners.

Funding sources, faced with overwhelming social issues, want to ensure efficient and effective programs and organizations. The funder's mantra—avoid duplication of services—is well known to

NEW DIRECTIONS FOR YOUTH DEVELOPMENT, NO. 114, SUMMER 2007 © WILEY PERIODICALS, INC.
Published online in Wiley InterScience (www.interscience.wiley.com) • DOI: 10.1002/yd.214

nonprofit managers. In addition, funding sources have a bird's-eye view of the nonprofit community, which allows them to see patterns and potentials that the individual nonprofit may not see. There is even some basis for the idea that funding sources tend to like the concept of collaboration and partnerships, sometimes over and above the utility of these activities.

A series of focus groups in November and December 2004 in Denver that looked at the relationship between collaboration and nonprofit effectiveness comprised two groups of nonprofit managers and one group of funding sources. The funding sources' view of collaboration diverged from the majority view of the other focus groups, made up of nonprofit managers. The funding sources felt strongly that it was an ongoing responsibility of foundations and other funding sources to maintain an emphasis on collaboration as part of their funding criteria, and many funding sources require collaboration as part of funding packages. "We see the big picture and can see where partnerships and collaborations make sense," is what one participant in the funding sources' group stated. This view contrasts with that of participants in the other focus groups, who felt that the nonprofit manager, not the funder, knows whether a particular collaboration would be fruitful. The managers further stated that they do not believe that funding sources are always aware of the true costs of collaboration, particularly in increased staff time. Further, the nonprofit managers felt that a funding inducement to collaborate, unless thoughtfully applied, could lead to mission and goal displacement on the part of nonprofit organizations.

A second class of stakeholders, nonprofits' clients, is broad and can range from individuals receiving services to the members of the public who benefit from the work the nonprofit does for the community. Summer Scholars has a strong partnership with the Denver Parks and Recreation Department. Its value is evident in the following statement from a parent: "It means a lot to me that my children are able to come to school and get extended education after school. They also get to go on field trips, such as the Museum of Nature and Science, skiing, and swimming. This is very convenient for me, and when I get off work, I am able to take my kids directly home."

COLLABORATION: LEVERAGING RESOURCES AND EXPERTISE 77

The third and most integral class of stakeholders whose perspective must be considered in the "why collaborate" discussion is an organization's potential collaborative partners. These organizations, whether public, private, or fellow nonprofit organizations, are the key. Stated more precisely, it is the relationships based in aligning missions and pursuing mutually beneficial goals among these organizations that are key.

Summer Scholars is an excellent exemplar of collaboration principles and practices. Summer Scholars is a large, multisite extended learning program that relies on comprehensive collaboration to accomplish its mission of improving the literacy and social skills of youth in Denver. Founded in 1994, Summer Scholars has served over fifteen thousand elementary school-aged students and their families with summer, after-school, and family literacy academic and enrichment programs. Summer Scholars is a community-based nonprofit organization with two significant collaborating partners: Denver Public Schools and, as earlier stated, the City of Denver's Parks and Recreation Department.

Today, Summer Scholars is an award-winning, year-round community literacy initiative partnering with twenty Denver Public Schools' elementary schools to provide 1,950 at-risk youth each year with high-quality reading and writing instruction and enrichment in the out-of-school-time hours. Summer Scholars' program components include summer literacy and recreation, school-year tutoring and enrichment, and year-round family literacy programs. All of Summer Scholars' programs are housed at partner elementary schools for the students and families that attend the schools. The program staff includes many regular employees of the school district, and significant effort is made to align and complement school-day instruction in Summer Scholars extended learning programs. The collaboration between Summer Scholars and Denver Public Schools began on a school-by-school basis. At each individual site, Summer Scholars and partner schools share specific responsibilities. The schools are responsible for providing space, recruiting students, selecting staff, and providing information on

student needs. Summer Scholars is responsible for program administration, staff and student supervision, training, activities, and
evaluation.

Summer Scholars and Parks and Recreation work together to provide recreation and enrichment to students in Summer Scholars'
tutoring programs. The collaboration began with the summer program. Afternoon recreation provided by Parks and Recreation at each
school site follows the morning academic instruction. Today, the collaboration also includes school-year after-school enrichment, with
Summer Scholars' and Parks and Recreation's staff working side by
side at schools to provide high-quality extended learning programs
for Denver children. Summer Scholars and Parks and Recreation staff
affectionately refer to their respective roles as the "academic geeks"
and the "jocks," in reflection of each organization's role and expertise. Summer Scholars and Parks and Recreation jointly supervise
each site, plan and implement staff training programs, and coordinate activities. Although each relationship is different, Summer
Scholars' collaborations with Denver Public Schools and Parks and
Recreation share many of the same successful components.

## Components of successful collaboration

### Shared priorities

Denver Public Schools' mission is to educate Denver's youth. A
high-quality tutoring program like Summer Scholars is an important asset to the district in meeting its goals. The Denver Parks and
Recreation mission includes providing recreation to Denver youth,
and through Summer Scholars, Parks and Recreation has ready
access to over seventeen hundred kids each year. Successful collaborations always have shared priorities.

### Combined resources

Partners in collaboration invest both financial and human resources
to ensure that collaboration will be successful. Without this invest-

ment, there will be a disparity of ownership that will lead to problems. Summer Scholars annually raises close to $2 million to support its programs for Denver Public School students, so it makes good economic sense for the district to devote resources to the program. Denver Public Schools provides all the space for programs, transportation services, and funding for teacher training, at a value of approximately $100,000 per year. Parks and Recreation brings close to $500,000 each year to the table as well.

### Institutional support and political will

Summer Scholars is fortunate to work closely and effectively with many individuals within the school district and city; however, effective collaboration also requires institutional support and the political will to develop this support. Summer Scholars is well recognized as a valuable community asset with the ability to influence policymakers, which has enabled the partnerships with the city and the school district to flourish and grow through several different mayors and superintendents.

Summer Scholars' founders, staff, and members of the board of directors are active and influential in the Denver community at large and are well known to the city council, mayor, and board of education. The relationship building that is essential to effective collaboration is ongoing at all levels.

Institutional support can and should be built through interpersonal relationships with key players who then have the potential to continue to reap rewards. Recently, one of the principals at a Summer Scholars partner school was promoted to another position within the district. The relationship with each school's principal is pivotal to the success of programs, so Summer Scholars made inquiries about the hiring process to request that the ability and willingness to work with community partners be a criterion for the selection of the next principal at this school. As it turns out, the point of contact was an area superintendent who was promoted and who also served as the lead principal for the summer program. Her knowledge, advocacy, and support of Summer Scholars are significant, so Summer Scholars is confident its concerns will be well addressed.

### Shared clarity of expectations

Summer Scholars' partnership with Parks and Recreation is very hands on, with lots of joint planning sessions and meetings. The partnership with Denver Public Schools is much less interactive and focuses on well-established roles and responsibilities for each group. The day-to-day management of programs is jointly shared by Summer Scholars and Parks and Recreation, whereas Summer Scholars bears more responsibility than does Denver Public Schools in actual program implementation. Both styles work well, and the key to both is clarity of expectations. For example, an important role for the principal of each Denver Public Schools partner school is to ensure that the resources and priorities are available to recruit students for the programs. The principals understand that this is their most fundamental responsibility to the program. Once the students are recruited and their participation is under way, the principal has little responsibility in the program's implementation. By contrast, Parks and Recreation supervisors participate in weekly meetings with Summer Scholars site coordinators to problem solve and plan day-to-day operations.

## Value added

The partnership of Parks and Recreation with Denver Public Schools adds significant value to services provided, and Summer Scholars adds value back to its partners. The ability to offer services in students' home school buildings provides a level of participation not otherwise likely. In addition, Summer Scholars provides high-quality teacher training that informs instruction on a daily basis throughout the city. Summer Scholars is able to offer recreation services to complement academics, and conversely, Parks and Recreation provides services with an academic component.

### Organizational identity and branding

Successful collaborators are "partner friendly." At Summer Scholars, every grant application, brochure, and newsletter describes the collaborations used to implement services, and all of the successes and awards are shared with partners. Collaboration is a part of Summer Scholars' organizational identity and brand identity. Recently the new superintendent of Denver Public Schools, Michael Bennett, rolled out a comprehensive plan for improving student achievement and the overall functioning of the district. Included in the plan was an objective to partner with community-based organizations for after-school and summer programs. Partnerships are part of the brand identity Bennett hopes to instill for the district.

## *Organizational effectiveness*

Collaborations among organizations will be more successful if the parties are independently effective in accomplishing their objectives. At the same time, a successful collaboration can improve organizational effectiveness. The demands of collaboration include accountability, openness, risk-taking, comprehensive planning, willingness to confront and deal with conflict, creative and appropriate allocation of resources including staff time, and shared ownership. These are characteristics of effective management, and collaboration can help ramp up these skills in the partners. Recent research that looked at the relationship between collaboration and nonprofit organizational effectiveness among Denver human service organizations found a strong relationship. Collaborative activities were a strong component in influencing effectiveness, second only to an organization's change in management skills. Other influencing factors are board of directors' performance and management practices. One might assume that this assistance is balanced according to organizational size, but this is not necessarily the case. Summer Scholars is a relatively small community-based organization, particularly when compared with the size of Denver Public Schools. Even so, Denver Public Schools Superintendent Bennett had this to say: "Summer Scholars' approach to staffing, programs, best practices, and teacher professional development is a model for the entire school district, and their results reflect the quality of this outstanding program." Dolores Moreno at Denver Parks and Recreation made a similar comment when she said that her agency's relationship with Summer Scholars "provides great learning resources for . . . staff even as it provides them the opportunity to serve 'the whole child.'"

NEW DIRECTIONS FOR YOUTH DEVELOPMENT • DOI: 10.1002/yd

### Common problems with collaboration

A lack of legitimate need is a common problem for many collaborations. Collaboration should be attempted only if there is a clear and present need that will be better met if organizations collaborate. Whereas many funding sources may require collaboration, a collaboration of convenience will only be window dressing and diminishes the value of true collaboration. Potential collaborating partners should consider how working together better serves the purpose of both organizations.

Sometimes incompatible organizational cultures make successful collaboration difficult to achieve. *Incompatible* refers to differences in processes, ownership, expectations, and quality of work. Summer Scholars began its collaboration with the school district one school at a time. At a school level, principals were motivated to help their students and willing to do the leg work necessary to help the program succeed. This bottom-up approach ensured that the initial stages of collaboration were between two groups with compatible organizational cultures. Had the effort been initiated with central administration, Summer Scholars' programs may have never been launched. Central Denver Public Schools administration would not have shared ownership with Summer Scholars' efforts in the same way individual schools did.

Not every collaborative effort undertaken by Summer Scholars has been successful. On these occasions, there has been a discrepancy in expectations, output, process, and quality of work.

Collaborations require significant investment of resources from all partners. Without mutual contribution of resources, shared ownership is difficult. The resources need not be equal but should represent an important financial commitment to the joint project.

An easy way to derail a collaboration is to disagree about who gets to call the shots or to overstep the bounds of authority. This can be prevented by clarifying expectations and roles at the outset and dealing with conflict quickly and openly. Parks and Recreation supervisors participate in Summer Scholars' weekly staff meetings for site coordinators who supervise both Summer Scholars and Parks and Recreation staff. This helps facilitate communication and addresses most issues that otherwise might have created conflicts.

## Steps to establishing or improving collaboration

Partners in collaboration need to clearly define and understand the need to be addressed by the collaboration, thus underscoring the legitimacy of the collaboration and each partner's interpretation of the problem the collaboration is addressing.

- *Confirm shared priorities.* Discuss each partner's mission and how the collaboration extends and complements both organizations' purposes.
- *Clarify differences in approach.* Identify differences in methods of service delivery and determine if the approaches can work together.
- *Build institutional support for collaboration.* Make sure the policy-makers and administrative and program staffs for both organizations are informed and supportive of the combined efforts.
- *Build on existing strengths.* Do not expect collaborating partners to provide a function in which they do not already have expertise. Instead, draw on and extend the strengths of both organizations to work together.
- *Foster the development of champions.* As with any effort, collaborations are well served by passionate, capable champions. Reinforce and appreciate the efforts made on behalf of the collaboration and constantly look to develop new champions.
- *Address problems as they arise.* Deal with conflict directly and apply the lessons learned to future efforts.
- *Know when to call it quits.* Not all collaborations will be successful. Continuing on in an unsuccessful partnership will take a toll on an organization's overall enthusiasm for collaboration. If a partnership is not working and cannot be fixed, call it quits.

In 2005, Summer Scholars was named the winner of the Excellence in Summer Learning award presented by the Center for Summer Learning at Johns Hopkins University. This national recognition was reinforcement to many program components at which Summer Scholars excels, including academic instruction, evaluation, and program administration. In addition, the award validated how Summer Scholars' collaborations have leveraged the resources and expertise of different types of institutions to best meet the needs of a community's youth. Summer Scholars' efforts with Denver Public Schools and Denver Parks and Recreation Department exemplify smart practices in collaboration and demonstrate the power of organizations working together.

### Note

1. Mattessich, P., & Monsey, B. (1993). *Collaboration: What makes it work.* St. Paul, MN: Amherst H. Wilder Foundation.

ANNE BYRNE *is executive director of Summer Scholars. Together with Delores Moreno from Denver Parks and Recreation, Byrne has presented information on collaboration at national youth development conferences.*

JANE HANSBERRY *is executive director of the Foundation for Human Enrichment.*

*Summer library reading programs provide opportunities for students of many ages and abilities to practice their reading skills and maintain skills they have developed during the school year.*

# 6

# Summer library reading programs

*Carole D. Fiore*

ALTHOUGH SUMMER LIBRARY READING PROGRAMS (SLRPS) started more than a century ago, the SLRPs of today are a key component in the creation of a nation of readers and thus of literate citizens. In the aggregate, SLRPs are an integral part of public library services. According to F. William Summers et al., "Virtually all public libraries (95.2 percent) provide summer reading programs for children. More children participate in public library summer reading programs than play Little League baseball. Moreover, these programs have been shown to play a definite role in children improving reading skills over the summer."[1]

Today, SLRPs are designed with intentional educational consequences. When summer library programs originated more than a century ago at the public library in Hartford, Connecticut, that was not necessarily the case. Since the origination of these recreational and educational summer library programs, numerous studies, most of them within the education field, have explored the value of reading over the summer.

NEW DIRECTIONS FOR YOUTH DEVELOPMENT, NO. 114, SUMMER 2007 © WILEY PERIODICALS, INC.
Published online in Wiley InterScience (www.interscience.wiley.com) • DOI: 10.1002/yd.215

## Early research

In her 1984 doctoral dissertation, Judith Menoher reported on previous studies that indicated that there is a direct relationship between ownership of books and the availability of books to students and their reading scores. She also reported that other studies found students who read more than ten books during the summer vacation made significant gains in reading ability over those who read less. Menoher's research found that reading books and magazines was among the top three activity choices that students in the fourth, sixth, and eight grades perceived helped them improve their reading ability.[2]

Other researchers endorse summer reading in whatever form it may take as a significant way to improve students' reading performance and document how summer library programs positively affect students' reading ability. Lesley Mandel Morrow states that correlation studies have found that children who read voluntarily or show an interest in books in early childhood or elementary and middle school grades achieve higher levels of reading on standardized tests. Children with early and frequent exposure to literature tend to develop sophisticated language structures and a sense of story structure. Literature-based summer library programs provide this exposure. These activities also help increase interest in learning to read.[3]

In 1984, Vivian Carter, children's librarian at the Normal (Illinois) Public Library, studied the effects of participation in public library summer reading programs on children's reading skills. Analysis of the data gathered by Carter during the study supports the following findings:

• Children who participate in the SLRP show an increase in vocabulary scores on post-testing whereas those who do not participate show a decrease.
• Children who participate in the SLRP show an increase in comprehension scores whereas those who do not participate show a decrease.[4]

NEW DIRECTIONS FOR YOUTH DEVELOPMENT • DOI: 10.1002/yd

## Summer learning and the effects of schooling

The most definitive study of the effects of summer library programs on the education of students was done by Barbara Heyns. Her landmark study, *Summer Learning and the Effects of Schooling*, was the first thorough investigation of summer learning. She followed sixth and seventh grade students in the Atlanta, Georgia, public schools through two academic years and an intervening summer.[5]

The most significant finding from the Heyns study is that the single summer activity that is most strongly and consistently related to summer learning is reading. Reading during the summer, whether measured by number of books read, time spent reading, or even the regularity of library usage systematically increases the vocabulary test scores of children. "Although unstructured activities such as reading do not ordinarily lend themselves to policy intervention," Heyns writes, "I will argue that at least one institution, the public library, directly influences children's reading. Educational policies that increase access to books, perhaps through increased library services, stand to have an important impact on achievement, particularly for less advantaged children."[6]

Heyns specifically found that socioeconomic status had little effect on reading achievement over the summer. Although reading tends to be patterned by family situation, the increases in summer learning are largely independent of a child's social class background.[7] She also found that children in every income group who read six or more books during the summer consistently gained more than children who read fewer books.[8] A conclusion from the Heyns study is, "The unique contribution of reading to summer learning suggests that increasing access to books and encouraging reading may well have substantial impact on achievement."[9] Both the number of books read and participating in a group where reading and literacy activities are valued add significantly to improved reading abilities, achievement, and attitudes.

## More recent findings

Although attention has been focused on finding out what happens to children's learning over the summer, no study has had the far-reaching impact of the Heyns study. According to recent research by Anne McGill-Franzen and Richard Allington, "Regardless of other activities, the best predictor of summer loss or summer gain is whether or not a child reads during the summer. And the best predictor of whether a child reads is whether or not he or she owns books."[10]

Research by Harris Copper and colleagues has helped the education community learn more about summer learning and summer learning loss. According to the authors, students appear at best to demonstrate no academic growth over the summer when there is no intervention. At worst, students appear to lose one month of grade-level-equivalent skills relative to national norms.[11]

McGill-Franzen and Allington also talk about summer setback. According to their research, children from low-income families are more prone to summer learning loss than children in middle- and upper-income families. As Alexander and Entwisle suggest, based on their research, summer learning loss is cumulative.[12] An annual "summer reading loss of three months accumulates to a crucial two-year gap by the time kids are in middle school, even if their schools are equally effective."[13]

## Reading versus library programs

Even though most summer library programs do not have maintaining students' reading skills as a specific goal, this turns out to be one of the benefits, and many summer programs do in fact have reading in their names. Whether known as the vacation reading club, summer reading club, vacation reading program, summer library program, or by some other name, these programs are similar. Having the word "reading" in the program name, however, does promote some expectations—and possible misconceptions—

on the part of the library user, whether adult or child, and the community as a whole.

Reading programs, as the name implies, emphasize reading. On hearing that a local library is sponsoring a reading program, many parents may think that the library is going to teach their child the skills needed to read. Libraries are devoted to promoting the lifelong love of reading, and the fact is that enjoyment is the chief motivator for learning skills. Numerous libraries throughout the United States are actively involved in adult and family literacy projects. Adult literacy programs are skills oriented; however, most family literacy programs are geared toward reading motivation rather than teaching reading skills for children of school age. Having reading as the key word in the program title may also lead to misinterpretation by library staff, the education community, and parents as well unless they come to understand the many aspects of reading and its relation to meaning, experience, imagination, interest, and discussion.

Library programs emphasize the many and varied resources that libraries have. Rather than focusing just on reading skills, library programs focus on the clients' introduction to thinking, learning, and sharing experiences with literature, and they can provide the welcome atmosphere where a child who does not excel in other areas can succeed. As the American Library Association National Library Week theme of several years ago says, "Kids who read succeed!" Library programs instill in children the love of reading for reading's sake rather than for a grade or prize. Library programs, when designed as noncompetitive activities, promote reading as an activity in which everyone can win.

Library programs are more diverse in nature than reading instruction or skills programs. They may feature new and developing technologies that libraries are adopting and the youth of our country are embracing, including computers, portable music players, gaming consoles, and the Internet. They are not as book centered as a reading program; summer library programs are able to help participants develop their visual literacy and language skills as well as give them practice in reading. Library programs tend to use the innate curiosity and information-seeking behaviors of the participants rather than

NEW DIRECTIONS FOR YOUTH DEVELOPMENT • DOI: 10.1002/yd

just prescribing a list of books from which to choose to read. Whether through a reading program or a library program, instilling a love of reading and providing participants with the skills necessary to survive in an information-saturated society is one of the end results of these programs. By allowing youth of our communities to see the value that a full-service library has to offer, not only are we creating the next generation of readers and library users, but we are also creating the next generation of library supporters.

In addition to instilling the love of reading in children and young adults, library programs promote cultural literacy, one of the goals of early twentieth-century programs. Through summer library programs, youth and their families are exposed not only to a variety of materials but also to the cultural resources of the community.

Although many schools and other educational agencies rely on required reading lists, many are discovering that library staff have the skill and ability to recommend many other developmentally and age-appropriate books for students to read during the summer. The education community is now realizing that having students participate in library programs in which the youth and their families are exposed to literature, folk and fairy tales, art, music, sports, food, languages, and other aspects of cultures with which they are both familiar and unfamiliar develops well-rounded citizens of the world. Although the social and cultural aspects of summer library programs are important, the educational value of these programs cannot be denied.

## Revisions and new designs

Previous research has shown that SLRPs are effective and could be more so when combined with a skill-oriented summer school; library programs that provided intentional learning opportunities are effective.

Stephen Krashen states that whereas direct instruction teaches the mechanics of reading, voluntary reading of literature is a powerful means of developing literacy, reading comprehension, writing style, vocabulary, and grammar.[14] Krashen defined *literature* as "any text that improves the lives of our students and helps them grow. . . . Literature is applied philosophy. It includes ethics, how we are supposed to live, and metaphysics, speculations on why we are here. Fiction is a very powerful way of teaching philosophy. Good stories help us reflect on our behavior and our lives."[15] A combined effort in which schools and libraries have separate yet distinct roles could help alleviate the problem of parents' misperceptions that SLRPs provide formal instruction.

Encouraging children to read is in the current and future interest of individual children, their families, the community, and the nation as a whole. Time spent reading would probably increase if the child enjoyed reading. Because research shows that good reading attitudes and skills are developed when children are young, it implies that parents and other primary caregiving adults should take an active interest in children's reading activities. Krashen states: "An important goal of literature is to encourage more reading and a wider range of reading among children. . . . Reading stories aloud to children is an important part of a literature program. There is strong and consistent evidence that reading to children builds language and literacy competence. . . . Reading stories helps indirectly as well, by stimulating an interest in reading."[16]

Encouraging children to read begins with reading aloud to children at the earliest age, discussing the books, and then continuing to do so even when they have acquired skills to read independently. A new report containing the most recent data indicates that 60 percent of three- to five- year olds were read to daily by a family member. This was not a significant increase from the previous report from four years ago where 58 percent of three- to five-year-olds received the same intervention.[17] Previous reports indicated that girls were more likely to have been read to than boys[18] Children who spend more time reading develop larger vocabularies and rank higher on standardized tests than peers who spend less time reading. A study reported in the *Reading Research Quarterly* finds that 90 percent of fifth grade students devoted only 1 percent of their free time to reading, 50 percent read for an average of four minutes or less per day, and 10 percent read nothing at all.[19]

NEW DIRECTIONS FOR YOUTH DEVELOPMENT • DOI: 10.1002/yd

Children who spend about one minute per day reading score in the tenth percentile on standardized tests. Children who spend about eleven minutes per day reading score in the fiftieth percentile. Children who spend approximately thirty-eight minutes per day score in the ninetieth percentile.[20]

## Practical applications

### Summer reading camps

One program established through the No Child Left Behind Act designed specifically to assist third grade students perform at a level that will enable them to be promoted to fourth grade is summer reading camps. Although not citing the work of the Center for Summer Learning, communications from the U.S. Department of Education cite the need for summer reading camps to counteract summer learning loss.[21] Although school districts have used summer schools for many years, the success of students enrolled in these programs has not been at the desired level. Summer school was looked on as punitive. Many of the children who attend mandatory summer school have few opportunities to read extensively in books that are "at their level and about topics that truly interest them. Our work suggests that if children have opportunities to listen to, discuss, and read books on topics they select, or books about the characters they love, they develop extensive background knowledge that can scaffold their independent reading and sustain their engagement. Summer school must provide interventions that can accomplish these goals."[22]

In Los Angeles in 2000, the Milken Family Foundation developed an eight-week reading summer day camp intervention program where disadvantaged first grade children attended reading camp instead of summer school. Within the context of summer camp, credentialed teachers taught reading to the campers for two hours per day. The remaining time was devoted to regular summer camp fun activities. These were supplemented with enrichment activities such as field trips to museums, aquariums, and cultural centers.

In 2003, this program was adapted to become the Summer Reading Achievers Project. The first Summer Reading Achievers program was offered through the auspices of the Atlanta Fulton Public Library. The public library reports that core to the success of the program is the collaboration with the public schools.[23] In 2004, this program was expanded to eleven diverse locations around the country. Although most of the programs are school based, they incorporate many of the activities that public libraries use in their summer library reading programs: reading logs, access to books, and parental involvement.[24]

### Summer Library Reading Partnership Program

At the same time that the U.S. Department of Education was developing its first summer reading camp, the State Library and Archives of Florida was developing the Summer Library Reading Partnership Program (SLRPP). Public libraries participating in this statewide program received federal Library Services and Technology Act grant funds based on the population of their service areas. Libraries partnered with local school districts, and together they targeted low-achieving third grade students. Libraries provided extra summer library activities both in the library and at the summer reading camp location. Whereas the schools focused on reading skills, libraries provided reading enrichment activities and materials.

### Bringing Libraries and Schools Together

Bringing Libraries and Schools Together (BLAST) is a school outreach program in which the Carnegie Public Library of Pittsburgh partners with the Pittsburgh Public Schools. Started in 2002, the program has expanded each year since then, with the school system asking the library system to visit more schools each year. Targeting students in kindergarten through fifth grade from schools in low-income neighborhoods, the BLAST staff visit each school in the program weekly. In 2003, the library was able to determine that 94 percent of the children in this outreach program were not registered for the in-house library program. Through this outreach experience, children in low-income neighborhoods were able to participate in a summer reading experience that they would otherwise not have had.

The library was complimented on the selection of books for this program. The books selected, while being age and developmentally appropriate, challenged the students to listen to and focus on what was being read. Activity sheets, though useful in some classrooms, were not used in others. Teachers made several suggestions to improve the program. In addition to suggesting that there be a field trip to take the students to the library, the teachers wanted the library to take the program to the schools twice weekly. They also suggested that each child be registered to get a library card.

### *Multnomah County Library*

Headquartered in Portland, Oregon, the Multnomah County Library is the oldest public library west of the Mississippi. One goal of Multnomah County Library's strategic plan is that it provide emergent-literacy and reading programs to youth of all ages. Another strategic goal states that library books and services support children and youth and satisfy their personal reading interests and educational needs. The summer reading program offered by this library system encourages readers and prereaders of all ages to experience and enjoy reading material of their own choice over the summer. The library program is designed to encourage reading over time. The program lasts for three months and encourages readers to select their own reading materials, with library staff assisting them to find what interests each participant most.

Rather than waiting for the youth of the community and their families to find the library and its programs, staff actively seek out programs and events to promote the summer reading program. In addition to annual participation in the Junior Rose Festival parade, the library has hosted kick-off celebrations at a local amusement park. The Multnomah County Library summer reading program has both television and radio sponsorship, resulting in hundreds of commercials airing over the course of the summer.

NEW DIRECTIONS FOR YOUTH DEVELOPMENT • DOI: 10.1002/yd

Over five hundred youth and adult volunteers log more than ten thousand hours annually. Their efforts help to manage this enormous project by distributing prizes, doing data entry, and maintaining prize inventories. By providing these volunteer opportunities, the library is allowing teens to contribute back to their community, an important part of youth development.

The library's LIBROS (*LIBR*ary *O*utreach in *S*panish; also the Spanish word for books) program, which promotes and connects Spanish-speaking patrons with library service, brings new life to the summer reading program. Working with in-house bilingual experts, the library is able to create program materials in Spanish. The library is also able to provide outreach to community organizations and summer-care sites to help Spanish-speaking babies, children, and teens all summer long. The library also provides materials, such as a parent-information sheet, in multiple languages: English, Spanish, Chinese, Russian, and Vietnamese.

In addition to involving the library's Early Childhood Resources office in the program, the library also has a "Books 2 U" program that takes the summer reading program directly to thousands of school-aged children at community centers, housing authority sites, schools, Boys' and Girls' Clubs, free-lunch sites, and other places where youth spend their time.

The Multnomah County Library Summer Reading Program enjoys a 99.8 percent approval rating from parents. The families not only like the prizes but say that the game motivates the family to read.

### Web-based programs

Public libraries all over the country offer special summer reading programs, and the libraries of the Big Apple are no exception. The Brooklyn Library, The New York Public Library, and the Queens Library have a jointly created Web site where children can locate a book that interests them. In addition to reading reviews written by other young people, they write their own review to inform their peers. Youth living in the New York metropolitan area can attend special events and earn prizes. Other summer library program Web sites provide interactive games as well as reading lists.

### Service learning programs

Whereas many libraries provide reading incentives, prizes, and rewards for reading, more and more libraries are incorporating service reading into their programs instead. Heifer International is an international organization that "works to end world hunger and save the earth."[25] Libraries and other organizations sign up. The Colchester-East Hants Regional Library in Truro, Nova Scotia, is one such library. Participating children gather sponsors who pledge money for how much time or how many books the children read. In 2004, the children at this Canadian library raised $2,000 that was given to Heifer International to buy livestock for developing countries.[26]

### Looking ahead

Libraries throughout the nation and the world continue to enhance their SLRP offerings. Libraries are using technology to track participation and allow for remote participation in these updated programs. In a world where libraries are competing for funding, they are partnering with other educational and child-serving agencies to better serve the youth of their communities and stretch the limited dollars that are available. More research is needed to document how libraries contribute to maintaining reading skills and the learning habit. With that documentation, summer library reading programs will become more accepted as a truly educational service that allows students to make the most of summer.

### Notes

1. Summers, F. W., Fraser, B. T., Landry, M., & Burnet, G. (1999). *Florida libraries are education: Report of a statewide study on the educational role of public libraries.* Tallahassee: School of Information Studies, Florida State University. P. iv.

2. Menoher, J. A. (1984). Factors affecting reading achievement retention over summer vacation. *Dissertation Abstracts International, 46*(01), DAI-A. (UMI No. AAT 8505585).

3. Morrow, L. M. (1987, December). Promoting inner-city children's recreational reading. *Reading Teacher, 41*(3), 266–274.

4. Carter, V. (1988, January). The effect of summer reading program participation of the retention of reading skills. *Illinois Libraries, 70*(1), 56–60.

5. Heyns, B. (1978). *Summer learning and the effects of schooling.* Orlando, FL: Academic Press.

6. Heyns. (1978). P. 161.

7. Heyns. (1978). P. 168.

8. Heyns. (1978).

9. Heyns. (1978). P. 172.

10. McGill-Franzen, A., & Allington, R. (2003, May-June). Bridging the summer reading gap. *Instructor, 112,* 18.

11. Cooper, H., Nye, B., Charlton K., Lindsay, J., & Greathouse, S. (1996, Fall). The effects of summer vacation on achievement test scores: A narrative and meta-analytic review. *Review of Educational Research, 66*(3), 227–268.

12. Alexander, K. L., Entwisle, D. R., & Olson, L. S. (2001). Schools, achievement, and inequality: A seasonal perspective. *Educational Evaluation and Policy Analysis, 23,* 171–191.

13. McGill-Franzen & Allington. (2003). P. 18.

14. Krashen, S. (1993). *The power of reading: Insights from the research.* Englewood, CO: Libraries Unlimited; Krashen, S. (2004, June 24). *Free voluntary reading: New research, applications, and controversies.* Paper presented at PAC5 (Pan-Asian Conference), Vladivostok, Russia. Retrieved June 8, 2004, from http://www.sdkrashen.com/articles/pac5/01.html.

15. Krashen, S. D. (1996). *Every person a reader: An alternative to the California Task Force Report on Reading.* Culver City, CA: Language Education Associates. Pp. 6–7.

16. Krashen. (1996). P. 7.

17. Forum on Child and Family Statistics. (2006). *America's children in brief: Key national indicators of well-being, 2006.* Retrieved May 9, 2007, from http://www.childstats.gov/americaschildren/summlist5.asp.

18. Federal Interagency on Child and Family Statistics. (2004). *America's children in brief: Key national indicators of well-being, 2004.* Washington, DC: Federal Interagency on Child and Family Statistics. For further information, go to http://childstats.gov.

19. Anderson, R., Fielding, L., & Wilson, P. (1988, Summer). Growth in reading and how children spend their time outside of school. *Reading Research Quarterly, 23*(3), 285–303.

20. Trelease, J. (2001). *The read aloud handbook* (5th ed.). New York: Penguin.

21. U.S. Department of Education. (2003, June 1). *The achiever: No child left behind.* Washington, DC: U.S. Department of Education. Retrieved October 28, 2004, from http://www.ed.gov/print/news/newsletters/achivere/2003/06012003.html.

22. McGill-Franzen & Allington. (2003). P. 58.

23. Huntington, B. (2003, August 14). Pilot summer reading program in Atlanta sponsored by the U.S. Department of Education. E-mail communication from the chair of the 2003 Collaborative Summer Library Program.

24. U.S. Department of Education. (2004). *No child left behind: Summer reading achievers.* Washington, DC: U.S. Department of Education; U.S. Department of Education. (2004). Summer reading program launched in 10 cities, one state." Press release. Washington, DC: U.S. Department of Education. Retrieved August 3, 2004, from http://www.ed.gov/news/pressreleases/2004/04/04082004a.html.

25. Heifer International. (2002). *Read to feed.* Retrieved November 14, 2004, from http://readtofeed.org/for_teachers_leaders_and_parents/.

26. Marsh, M. L. (2004, November 12). E-mail message to public libraries, young adults, and children.

CAROLE D. FIORE, *an independent library consultant, is president of Training and Library Consulting and author of Fiore's Summer Library Reading Program Handbook (2005).*

*This chapter highlights best practices from the field
by outlining the approach of Building Educated
Leaders for Life to using evaluation data for continuous program improvement.*

# 7

# Using evaluation to improve program quality based on the BELL model

*Earl Martin Phalen, Tiffany M. Cooper*

BUILDING EDUCATED LEADERS FOR LIFE (BELL) prioritizes a rigorous approach to evaluation and is committed to continuous program improvement. Several principles for effective practice inform the conduct of evaluation at BELL and serve to continuously strengthen the organization's service to children and communities. In this chapter, we highlight best practices from the field by out-lining BELL's approach to using evaluation data for continuous program improvement, including (1) working with intended users throughout the evaluation process, (2) reporting findings with program-relevant timing, and (3) making and supporting explicit recommendations for the next program cycle.

---

## BELL

Founded in 1992 by students at Harvard Law School, BELL is a national not-for-profit organization whose mission is to increase the educational achievements, self-esteem, and life opportunities

NEW DIRECTIONS FOR YOUTH DEVELOPMENT, NO. 114, SUMMER 2007 © WILEY PERIODICALS, INC.
Published online in Wiley InterScience (www.interscience.wiley.com) • DOI: 10.1002/yd.216

of elementary school children living in low-income urban communities. BELL operates two award-winning out-of-school-time programs: BELL After School and BELL Summer. Since 1992, BELL has provided exceptional educational opportunities to more than twenty thousand children and families.

The BELL After School program operates weekdays for two and a half hours per day in school-based sites. Each day, students (who, once enrolled, are called scholars) receive a nutritious snack and participate in one hour of literacy tutoring and one hour of math tutoring in small groups of no more than eight scholars per tutor. The BELL Summer program operates for five days per week, eight hours per day, in school-based sites. Three hours each morning, Monday through Thursday, are committed to reading, writing, and math instruction. Afternoons include structured enrichment activities such as music, art, drama, and physical education. "Mentor Friday" ends each week with inspirational guest speakers, cultural presentations, field trips, and community service projects. At every school site, BELL's programs are managed by a site manager, who establishes partnerships with principals, teachers, and parents to ensure that all children receive the attention and specialized support they need to excel. Academic instruction using research-based literacy and math curricula aligned to national and regional standards is provided by certified teachers and highly trained college students and community members. Program staff commit to at least a six-month tenure with BELL so that strong mentoring relationships are formed with scholars.

## Evaluation at BELL

BELL has been engaged in formal evaluation, internally and externally, for more than five years and has built internal evaluation capacity by investing in a specialized full-time evaluation team. Evaluation is centered on outcome measurement, focusing on the program's goals for scholars and families: improve academic performance in reading, writing, and math; enhance self-concept, confidence in abilities, and attitude toward learning; develop social skills, leadership abilities, and perception of one's self as a contributing member of a community; and engage scholars' parents as facilitators and advocates of their education. Measures include standardized preprogram and postprogram assessments, surveys, focus groups, and observations. In addition, BELL collects feedback about service delivery from internal and external stakeholders and monitors program implementation for quality assurance.

Evaluation findings are discussed with BELL's evaluation advisory board, governing board, senior management team, and regional program staff to determine the most effective elements of the program model and to identify areas for improvement. As part of a continuous program improvement model of evaluation, BELL uses the data to refine program implementation and replicate successful elements of the services and operations. For example, in 2002 BELL added a phonics curriculum to the two-hour literacy block in the summer schedule based on scholars' relatively smaller improvement in that area compared with other important reading skills. BELL's use of data for program improvement has been recognized as a best practice in the out-of-school-time field by the Promising Practices in After-School consortium sponsored by the Academy for Educational Development.

During the summers of 2004 and 2005, BELL participated in an independent third-party evaluation to measure the extent to which BELL Summer contributes to learning gains of children in low-income communities. This study used an experimental design, considered the gold standard in evaluation methods, and will offer the field the first experimental evidence of a multisite summer program.

Relating evaluation data to program improvement relies on having the right information at the right time. It starts with asking the right questions and ends with reporting information in a way that makes recommendations explicit and available in time to improve in the next program cycle. In addition to timing, evaluations should be conducted in accordance with well-designed plans and professional standards. This is best done by working on the front end with those who intend to use the evaluation information for program improvement and on the back end, making evaluation reporting and use a regular part of the program cycle.

## Working with intended users

Leveraging evaluation activities to obtain the right information involves working with intended users. Although working with stakeholders is standard practice in any evaluation,[1] working with *intended users* is a specific approach pioneered by Michael Quinn Patton as part of his Utilization-Focused model of program evaluation.[2] His approach begins with the premise that evaluations should be judged by their utility and actual use, where *use* concerns how real people experience evaluation and apply evaluation findings. Patton suggests that a utilization-focused evaluator works with clearly identified intended users who are responsible for applying evaluation findings and implementing recommendations; the evaluator also ensures that their values frame the evaluation. Under this theory, the evaluator works within a highly personal and situational environment. She or he develops a relationship with the intended users to help them determine the details of an evaluation that will be useful to them.

### Identifying intended users

Patton urges evaluators to consider that *people* use evaluation information, not organizations, and calls this the "personal factor."[3] The personal factor represents the leadership, interest, and enthusiasm of intended users. Finding primary intended users involves narrowing the list of all potential evaluation stakeholders (those who make decisions or desire information about a program) to those with responsibility for operating or supporting the program and who need evaluative information to support their work.

To support continuous program improvement at BELL, evaluation activities relate directly to the interests of each program support function, including student enrollment, staff recruitment, staff training, purchasing and distribution, and curriculum. Activities also focus on the interests of program managers, including site managers and regional directors. The decision to add a phonics curriculum to BELL's main summer instructional curriculum, for example, was facilitated by the evaluator but driven by BELL's director of curriculum and instruction. Individuals selected to par-

NEW DIRECTIONS FOR YOUTH DEVELOPMENT • DOI: 10.1002/yd

ticipate in program evaluation efforts within each department are identified in part by senior leadership, whose goal in selecting delegates is to support use.

## Involving intended users

**Getting intended users on board.** Once the group is narrowed to primary intended users, their information needs must direct the evaluation. Active involvement of users in the entire evaluation process will facilitate use later. Actively involving intended users includes training users in use, preparing the groundwork for use, and reinforcing the intended utility of the evaluation during its focusing, designing, and reporting phases.

Intended users, like stakeholders broadly, are not always eager to be involved. Individual reactions and openness to evaluation will vary and are likely to include those who see evaluation involvement as a burden and those who will fear it as a judgment of their performance. Getting intended users to support and participate in program evaluation requires, and is completely dependent on, alleviating any such apprehensions.

The Discrepency Evaluation Model (DEM), pioneered by Malcolm Provus, arises out of attempts to respond constructively to apprehensions regarding evaluation. In this model, an evaluation starts with a description of how a program *should* be (the standard), which often happens by breaking the program into its major activities, functions, or components through an input-process-output analysis. The evaluation continues with an investigation of whether the program *actually is* that way (the performance). Finally, a comparison of the standard against the performance provides information about any "discrepancy."[4] The DEM evaluator allows the intended users to establish the standard and to judge the discrepancy. For example, during the evaluation planning process, the director of curriculum and instruction at BELL established that she wanted to observe a ten-point improvement in phonics skills among program participants, and when the outcome data reflected an eight-point improvement, the director judged that to be too small and decided that phonics instruction needed to improve.

With this model, the evaluator serves as the facilitator. This role permits a constructive response to technical, political, organizational, and emotional problems that could be encountered when involving intended users or any group of stakeholders. The important element of this model is that the standard is not set by "experts" but instead by those responsible for program management and implementation. It is particularly important, under the assumptions of this model, that the intended users choose and commit themselves to the standard pertinent to their circumstances, even though they may rely on expert input.

*Involving intended users throughout.* Theory and practice suggest that it is essential to involve the intended users in first establishing evaluation questions. One best practice with regard to initially engaging intended users is to interview them to find out what they would like to know about the program.[5] What questions or concerns do they have? What are their perceptions of the program? How would they change the program if they had the opportunity? This process allows the intended users to generate the evaluation questions before or during the DEM process of establishing the standards. To judge the thoughtfulness and importance of their questions, those leading the evaluation should ask what the intended users would do with the answers to particular questions. The goal at this phase of the process is to identify high-yield evaluation questions so that the evaluation provides the right information. At BELL, intended users are trained to understand that appropriate evaluation questions are ones that reduce uncertainty.

It is likewise important to involve the intended users in the design, methods, and measurement decisions. The data collection instruments and reported outcomes have to be credible to the users. For example, those responsible for the evaluation should consider with the intended users how they will perceive and use observation versus survey data or how they would respond to various sample sizes or response rates. At BELL, for example, responses regarding phonics curriculum implementation from teacher surveys are viewed as exponentially more credible than information from a random sample of observations. Involving intended users at this stage, even though they might not be technical or evaluation experts, adds validity to the study because they are the program implementation experts.

Finally, it is important to involve intended users in data interpretation. The aim is to combine the results of data analysis done by the evaluator with value statements, criteria, and standards established by the intended users in order to produce the conclusions, judgments, and recommendations. Intended users must be actively and directly involved in interpreting findings and generating recommendations.

## *Reporting as a component of the program cycle*

The right information, obtained through the process described above, must be delivered in a readable, user-friendly format and must be timed to align with decision making. Effective reporting addresses several interrelated dimensions: timing, content, and follow-through.

Delivery time lines should be worked out, with the objective of making findings available at a specified time; generally the timing is roughly tied to the life cycle of the program. BELL, for example, begins planning for its summer on December 1 of the previous year. The planning process is facilitated by a formal project plan with the national operations manager serving as the project manager for each region. The summer project plan includes clear deliverables and time lines for all areas of regional operations (that is, student enrollment, staff recruitment, staff training, purchasing, and distribution) as well as national support functions (curriculum, evaluation, finance, and development). An early task in the plan is to "consider lessons learned," which are derived directly from evaluation data.

Evaluation findings from the previous summer play a key role in the planning process. These data take the form of a lessons-learned report issued to the senior management and key functional areas in November before the launch of the formal project plan in December. This report is informed by feedback from key internal and external stakeholders, including survey data from parents, outcome data relating to scholars, and survey and interview data from the teaching and management staff. Once intended users have judged the discrepancy between the standards they set and performance, recommendations are discussed, and intended users make agreements about actions. The final report puts actionable items and other recommendations at the front to make them explicit. The actionable items have specific assigned ownership: for example, the name of the individual who is responsible for pursuing the new phonics curriculum and supporting its implementation.

Senior management buy-in goes a long way toward supporting a culture of learning and establishing accountabilities around agreed-on actions. The same senior managers who identified department delegates for involvement in the evaluation process are the ones who manage follow-through on actions and accountabilities. This follow-through is the final step that makes evaluation use for continuous improvement possible.

## *Conclusion*

Best practices for using evaluation data for continuous program improvement come from theory and effective implementation at BELL. BELL's successful use of data for improvement is evidenced by the consistently strong outcomes for the students it serves as well as increased efficiency and satisfaction related to service delivery that has supported the replication of BELL's programs nationally. BELL scholars consistently demonstrate significant grade-equivalent gains in reading and math skills and significant improvements in self-esteem and social skills. Feedback has been used to effectively replicate services in four large urban regions while ensuring that programs achieve the same or better outcomes for every child served.

Best practices include (1) identifying intended users, typically individuals responsible for various program functions (for example, curriculum); (2) involving intended users in identifying evaluation questions, developing the evaluation plan, and interpreting data; (3) providing evaluation findings in an organized and timely manner based on planning for the next program cycle; (4) making recommendations explicit and assigning ownership; and (5) having an organizational mechanism for following up on the execution of agreed-on recommendations.

### Notes

1. Joint Committee on Standards for Educational Evaluation. (1994). *The program evaluation standards: How to assess evaluations of educational programs.* Thousand Oaks, CA: Sage.

2. Patton, M. Q. (2000). Utilization-focused evaluation. In D. L. Stufflebeam & G. F. Madaus (Eds.), *Evaluation models: Viewpoints on educational and human services evaluation* (2nd ed., pp. 425-438). Norwell, MA: Kluwer.

3. Patton. (2000).

4. Steinmetz, A. (2000). The discrepancy evaluation model. In D. L. Stufflebeam & G. F. Madaus (Eds.), *Evaluation models: Viewpoints on educational and human services evaluation* (2nd ed, pp. 127-144). Norwell, MA: Kluwer.

5. Fitzpatrick, J. L., Sanders, J. R., & Worthen, B. R. (2004). *Program evaluation: Alternative approaches and practical guidelines* (3rd ed.). Boston: Pearson.

EARL MARTIN PHALEN *is cofounder and CEO of BELL (Building Educated Leaders for Life).*

TIFFANY M. COOPER *is chief program officer of BELL and a doctoral candidate in educational research, measurement, and evaluation at Boston College.*

*The research is clear: All children need summer programs to prevent learning loss. But how do we find the resources to pay for them?*

# 8

# Finding the resources for summer learning programs

*M. Jane Sundius*

AS OTHER CHAPTERS in this issue make clear, there is abundant research identifying and quantifying the summer learning losses that result from the long American summer vacation. We have known for one hundred years that students without learning opportunities lose academic ground in the summer months.[1] And because poor children tend to have fewer opportunities to keep learning over the summer, their summer learning losses are greater than those of their more affluent peers.[2] Global economic competition makes these academic losses more and more expensive for our country to bear, and they are not the only negative outcome of inadequate summer programming for kids. On top of academic losses is the lack of supervision that too often occurs when parents' work puts far too many kids at risk for harmful social, emotional, physical, and physiological outcomes. And without school lunches and breakfasts, kids also suffer nutritional deficits.[3]

Although the research has unambiguous implications for American education—namely, that more children need learning opportunities in the summer—how and when policymakers, educators, and youth service providers will fashion appropriate programming

⚛WILEY
**InterScience®**
DISCOVER SOMETHING GREAT

NEW DIRECTIONS FOR YOUTH DEVELOPMENT, NO. 114, SUMMER 2007 © WILEY PERIODICALS, INC.
Published online in Wiley InterScience (www.interscience.wiley.com) • DOI: 10.1002/yd.217

are much less obvious. At the root of this issue is the need to vastly increase and stabilize resources available for summer programming. As the director of the education and youth development program at a private foundation with a long-standing commitment to increased after-school and summer school programming, I have seen firsthand how inadequate and highly variable funding limits the spread of summer learning programs and contributes mightily to the continued existence of summer learning losses.

In this article, I will focus on funding; in particular, I will make the case that two key strategies necessary to secure sustainable increases in funding involve national advocacy and public will-building efforts and comprehensive, collaborative planning at the local level. More specifically, it is critical to recognize that getting to scale will require that programs do something more than chase small programmatic grants from private funders to sustain themselves. In addition and more important in the long run, they need to advocate for large investments in summer learning opportunities by public systems. The conversation about sustainability, therefore, should be less about finding grants to continue program operations and more about ensuring that summer is a public priority. This article is an attempt to bring attention to the need to think strategically about funding and to outline a set of actions aimed at reducing the summer funding shortfall.

### *Where are we now?*

The good news is that there is evidence of large and steady increases in programming and funding for both the public and private sector summer learning opportunities. In 2000, summer school for failing students was required by more than 25 percent of all school districts. More than half of the fifty largest school districts offer summer programming[4]; by some estimates, this represents a near doubling of public school summer programming over the past twenty-five years.[5] Over the eight-year period from 1991 to 1998, the percentage of Title I public elementary schools that used this compensatory funding for summer programming rose from 15 to

41 percent.[6] The total number of children attending public summer schools is estimated to be five million, or close to 10 percent of public school children.[7] Evidence about participation of children nationwide who attend summer programs run by other public agencies like recreation departments is difficult to find, as are statistics about the growth of nonprofit and for-profit summer programs. One estimate from the American Camp Association reports that the number of day camps has increased by 90 percent over the past twenty years and that currently more than eleven million children attend day and resident camps each summer.[8]

These trends are not surprising given increased educational standards and working parents' needs for summer supervision for children. Although summer programs are increasing, there has been scant attention to growing summer opportunities in a systematic, comprehensive, sustainable, and equitable manner. Nor have most public summer programs been designed in ways that truly address summer learning loss issues; they are remedial, rather than enriching, one-shot as opposed to multisummer, running for only a couple of weeks rather than a month or more, and with curricula that are too haphazardly planned to provide significant help to children.

In most American communities, public summer schools are remedial programs or special education efforts available to some, but not all, students. Not all of these public school programs are free: high school-level credit recovery programs, for example, often charge students fees. Elsewhere in many communities, nonprofit youth organizations like the YMCA and Boys' and Girls' Clubs develop summer programs that, depending on funding, are offered for free or at a modest fee. These programs typically vary in availability from year to year, depending on funding, and seldom have enough slots for all the children who want to participate. The summer program landscape also includes fee-based day and residential camps that provide all sorts of enrichment opportunities, but these full-fare programs can cost parents several hundred dollars a week and result in a five-figure bill for a full summer of supervision and learning.

NEW DIRECTIONS FOR YOUTH DEVELOPMENT • DOI: 10.1002/yd

As this sketchy description of the summer program landscape demonstrates, we do not know with any degree of precision the number and kinds of programs that exist currently, what programs are most effective, and what they cost. Nor have there been community-, state-, or federal-level efforts to assess the gap between available programs and the summer needs of children in a given city or school district. Limited documentation of the summer landscape is partly the result of educational inertia and inattention, but also stems from the difficult nature of data collection about supply and demand. As the preceding paragraph demonstrates, summer program providers are numerous, diverse, and are not linked by any one organization or network. The programs they offer vary in duration, intensity, and number of participant slots, not only from provider to provider but also from year to year.

The complexity of determining current program supply is matched by the difficulty of assessing program demand. This is because children have needs that vary depending on their family context, parental work, school performance, and personal interests. At present, some families would say that their children do not need summer programs and others would say that they need full-time supervision for their children. Thus, as is true in the current after-school arena, the number of programs needed is not simply the number of children. Instead, it is the number who want or need access to programs.

On the national level, advocacy, education, research, and training efforts are beginning to rectify these problems, but they are underdeveloped and typically subsumed within the more prominent after-school advocacy agenda. Organizations like the After-school Alliance and the National Institute on Out-of-School Time all speak to the importance of summer programs but, as a secondary agenda item, well behind the needs of after-school programming. Although total federal spending for summer is not well measured, it appears that federal funding streams mirror this hierarchy. Whereas federal Title I, 21st Century Community Learning Centers, and No Child Left Behind Supplemental Educational Services are increasingly being used to fund summer programs, most of these funding streams appear to be dedicated to school-year programming. As of yet, there is no national funding stream dedicated to summer programming, although there are the beginnings of an effort to develop such a source of funds.

In summary, there is evidence that summer programs in school districts and private recreation and camp providers are increasing in number. Some evidence also exists of increased advocacy and federal funding for summer programs. However, there is a dearth of information about the current supply of programs and the demand and funding for programs. Finally, little exists in the way of new or promising revenue streams to finance summer learning on a universal scale.

## Building a public consensus about summer learning and a national summer learning advocacy effort

How do we move forward given the current piecemeal, inadequate, and highly variable state of summer funding? The most critical step in increasing sustainable sources of funding for summer learning opportunities is to develop a public consensus about what it will take to make summer a time that benefits all children. Most Americans view summer as a critical part of childhood, one that gives kids time for creative, regenerative, and different-from-the-school-year experiences. Many parents see summer as a time to customize their child's education and life experiences in very personal ways: giving them time to catch their breath, catch up and move forward with school, relationships with out-of-town relatives, hobbies, other interests and passions.

I would argue that there is much to be said in favor of this summer vision from a developmental, learning, and family perspective. The problem is not so much that this view of summer is inappropriate or harmful; it is that too many children do not have experiences that match it. Furthermore, those who do not have these experiences are generally children with great academic, social, economic, or personal needs. They are the children whose families cannot or do not provide summer experiences that help them grow personally and positively. Children's summer academic losses, nutritional deficits, and risk-taking behaviors are evidence that this wonderful notion of summer does not apply to all children.

Thus, the work of those who care about youth and summer learning losses is not to convince Americans that their views must be discarded in favor of a standardized, national summer school or program policy; it is to call for an expansion of opportunities that help all kids realize the American notion of summer. Whereas such a policy must address the issue of summer slide head-on, it must also be constructed in a way that embraces American beliefs about summer and builds on them to the benefit of children. Equally important, it must allow a diversity of programming and options for parents, adequate and equitable access to enrichment opportunities, and a way of ensuring that all kids benefit, not just those with socially or economically advantaged families.

Without a more widely held understanding of and commitment to improving summer learning opportunities, America is unlikely to improve children's summer outcomes. School systems, especially those with underperforming students, are likely to continue their too-little, too-late remedial approaches to summer learning. Youth service and summer camp providers will continue to offer summer enrichment opportunities, but are unlikely to be able to ensure access to all children in need.

Developing this message and building the infrastructure to deliver it nationwide are critically important jobs of summer learning advocates and public and private providers of summer programs. To be successful at these important and large tasks, summer learning must become the sole responsibility of a set of strong advocacy and educational organizations. Whereas education, after-school, juvenile justice, and child welfare agencies and organizations can and should be called to support this effort, these agencies alone are unlikely to help summer learning achieve the kind of prominence it requires to move policy and funding decisions. They are bound first to address their primary missions and are likely to be only ancillary supporters of summer learning. As has been the case with the after-school movement, the summer learning agenda must be carried forward by a host of national advocacy, research, training, and technical assistance organizations.

NEW DIRECTIONS FOR YOUTH DEVELOPMENT • DOI: 10.1002/yd

Financing for new organizations and funds to strengthen those that currently exist are both critically needed and an opportunity for private foundations that work to improve children's life outcomes. Although funding model summer camps and other summer programs are valuable endeavors with short-term payoffs, funding to support message development, program effectiveness, and efficiency research, communications, and advocacy efforts is more likely to achieve dramatic change over the longer term. If the summer learning agenda is to be successful, advocacy organizations, practitioners, and researchers must increasingly make this case to their funders.

## Developing local plans to implement comprehensive summer programming

While the key to vastly increasing support for summer programs is a national campaign that leads to a full understanding of children's summer learning needs, that work will not guarantee a large number of new, high-quality summer programs. In addition, American communities will need intensive local planning efforts if they are to create the necessary programs. Taking a cue from localities that have built and expanded after-school programs citywide—Boston, Baltimore and Los Angeles, for example—it is clear that community-level needs assessments and asset mapping can help to identify critical needs, unearth valuable resources, and develop an action plan. They are a first step for cities and localities trying to build and connect comprehensive sets of summer programs.

Communities must draw on all of their resources to solve the summer learning problem, rather than relying on one organization or agency. In large part, all youth-serving agencies and organizations must be a part of a local plan because no one public agency is currently equipped or predisposed to offer the range of programming that is required if we are to make the American notion of summer a reality. Schools are driven ever more exclusively by the need to produce academic results, and their summer programs typically reflect this myopia. A singular academic focus is especially common

in systems that serve a large number of poor or academically struggling children; in those systems, funding and the demands of standardized test preparation have led to shocking declines in physical
education, art, music, and other course offerings beyond the core
academic curriculum. This is not to say that schools have a minor
role in building systems of summer programming. Schools are
unique in that they are the public agency that has responsibility for
reaching all children; they also typically have the largest budget and
often have access to funds that other public agencies do not.

Despite their primary importance, schools cannot provide all of
the educational programming that children need. Nor can other public agencies. Public departments of recreation may squeeze in a summer reading program, and libraries may schedule a physical activity
period to break up the day at their summer reading camp, but none
of our public agencies is in the business of providing programs with
the full range of physical, cognitive, social, and recreational opportunities that are key components of an effective summer program.

Nongovernmental agencies, including youth service and summer
camp providers, have similar limitations. Whereas many offer programs with a broader scope than their public agency counterparts,
few of these can provide the intensive cognitive programming that
some children require to stay on grade level. Perhaps even more
significant is that none of these organizations can provide programs
on the scale that is required if all children are to have access. With
their creativity, enrichment expertise, and ability to attract diverse
audiences of children, these providers have much to add to a locality's plan for summer programming. But like their public agency
counterparts, they can be only a piece of the summer program quilt.

There is another practical reason that communities will need to
pull all youth providers together if they are to build a comprehensive set of summer opportunities. Simply put, summer programming will require an enormous amount of human and financial
capital if it is to be available to all children. Cities and other localities will need the staff and resources of both public and private
youth organizations if they are to meet the needs of all of their
children. And while funding must increase, it is a sure bet that it

will not increase enough to support a wholly new system of opportunities for kids. Maximizing the substantial resources that communities have already mustered to serve children in the summer makes sense from service provision and cost-efficiency standpoints. Simply put, increased summer programming will most likely be the result of a hearty "push" for additional funds and a forceful "squeeze" of existing youth programming dollars.

In making this case for extensive local planning, I do not mean to suggest that there has been no planning and partnering in American communities. In many places, and for many years, public-private partnerships, collaborations among youth service providers, and joint ventures between public agencies have been expanding summer program opportunities for children and youth. But in most places, these efforts are at best isolated ones that do not take as their mission serving all of a locality's children for the long term. The task of planning for all children throughout the summer is not an easy one, especially because the resources to do so are not in hand. And even when a city or locality decides to take on this effort, it is not easily or quickly accomplished. Nonetheless, it is essential to building a comprehensive, efficient set of programs for children.

## An example from Baltimore

The planning undertaken in Baltimore in 2005 is an example of the possibilities and challenges involved in a recent citywide effort to increase summer learning opportunities. The Baltimore effort began with the leadership of its public school system, the Center for Summer Learning, and the Safe and Sound Campaign, the city's leading after-school advocate. The five-year goal of this planning effort was to find a way to provide summer school to all interested children and to wrap enrichment programming around all of those school-like programs to meet children's nonacademic needs.

The process was carefully planned and began auspiciously. The group identified the leadership of the Baltimore City Public School System (BCPSS) as critical: not only was BCPSS the sole agency

whose mission was to reach all children, it was also the most powerful and resource-rich public agency in the city. The three principal
partners also invited a wide array of stakeholders to the discussions
and provided a good deal of information about summer learning
losses and effective program models. In addition, they scheduled a significant amount of time for group discussion and consensus building.

Despite these careful planning efforts, it was not easy sailing.
There were latecomers to the process who felt excluded and did not
want to buy into the group's recommendations. And although there
was a good deal of consensus about the importance of summer
learning and the need for more programming, there was much less
agreement about program priorities, the appropriate balance
between academics and enrichment, which outcomes were most
important for children, and which children should be targeted to
attend the first set of programs.

At the heart of many disagreements was underlying skepticism
that the effort would succeed, that it was the beginning of a long-
term plan to make Baltimore a place where summer programs
were universally available. Thus, the question of which children
should be eligible took on additional significance because participants believed that there might not be additional program slots in
the future. Similarly, participants believed that the transitory nature
of past summer programs would continue to plague future programs. As a result, discussions often centered on the upcoming summer, its programs and funding, rather than on a longer-term view.
The short supply of current funding also figured prominently in the
group's calculus. With current funding limitations firmly in mind,
many participants found it difficult to plan for greatly increased levels of service in the future.

Although Baltimore did not implement universal summer programming in 2005, its planning initiative did help it move summer
learning forward in a number of important ways. First, by establishing a long-term inclusive planning process, it raised the level
of awareness and understanding about the need for comprehensive
programming and the shared nature of the solution. Simply put, it
communicated that all of the city's children needed access to pro-

gramming and all of the city's youth service providers—public and private—were a part of the solution. Second, it set a goal for comprehensive programming within five years and began the longer work of building a consensus among program providers about the characteristics and goals of summer programs. Finally, it increased 2005 programming above the level of 2004 and set priorities about who would receive these programs.[9]

What Baltimore did not accomplish is also instructive. Yet to be completed is a system for matching afternoon enrichment programming with school-like morning programs. This is critically important if summer programming is to meet the broader social, physical, and nonacademic needs of children. Also still on the to-do list is a public education effort that clearly communicates the importance of summer learning opportunities and the harm caused by summer cognitive, social, and nutritional neglect to Baltimore citizens.

And finally, the planning effort has yet to tackle the funding questions associated with increased programming. For example, Title I funds provided a large infusion of funds in 2004 and 2005; however, this funding stream is not likely to be used once the city moves to more universal programming. That is because Title I dollars cannot pay for programs that non-Title I children also receive. The federal logic is that once an intervention becomes universal, it is no longer targeted for at-risk children and cannot be paid for by Title I. Beyond the funding source, the planning group must also determine how much additional funding is needed and how much of current funding for summer programs can be used toward this effort. This task will involve pushing public and private sources for additional funding and squeezing dollars out of existing programs by redirecting, collaborating, and partnering.

## Conclusion

Although research supporting the need for universal access to summer learning opportunities is clear and convincing, there has been no clarion call for increased programming and resources. At the root of this issue is a misconception about the summer experiences of many children. Far from being the regenerative, creative period that is so much a part of our collective American consciousness, summer is too often a period of neglect, when opportunities for children to develop new skills and talents and passions are squandered and children fall backward, instead of moving forward.

How do we get from our current piecemeal summer learning approach to one that allows us to realize the real opportunity that summer offers? My experiences in Baltimore and as a funder have led me to believe that two key strategies are essential to transforming the current state of summer programming.

The first involves a national education, advocacy, and public will-building effort. Summer learning advocates and program providers must develop a clear and convincing message that grows out of American's current notions of summer to make the case for a significant expansion of summer learning opportunities. To bolster the argument, advocates will also have to summarize and communicate the research that documents the current reality of children's summer experiences and the negative outcomes that are the result of summer neglect. In addition, they must build an organizational infrastructure that will communicate this message, putting it in front of policymakers, educators, parents, and other citizens. In short, the goal of this first step is to build a national consensus about children's summer learning needs.

Second, this national communications effort must be supplemented with local, intensive, collaborative, and long-term planning. Communities must begin a mapping process that documents available services and service gaps and that identifies resources in hand and resource needs. With a clear sense of their current summer landscapes, community stakeholders must then move on to build inclusive, public-private program and funding collaboratives. The task of these groups is to develop plans for expanded multi-dimensional, coordinated programs that can ultimately serve all of their communities' children. The inclusive nature of collaboratives is critical. If they do not include a wide array of youth providers and public agencies, communities are unlikely to create summer program plans that offer a full range of learning opportunities. Broad-based groups are also more likely to pull in and efficiently use existing resources and have the clout to attract funding to support large program expansions.

Private foundations can play a key role by supporting communications and planning efforts. Funding for either or both of these strategies is an ideal investment for private foundations. Foundation dollars are not sufficient to cover the cost of large program expansions. This is not to say that direct program costs should not be supported by philanthropic funding but that investments in communications, advocacy, and planning efforts are a more likely long-term solution to inadequate program funding.

Finally, as Baltimore's experience shows, these tasks are not likely to be easily or quickly accomplished. But they have the potential to transform the summer landscape and the learning outcomes for many American children. Far from requiring that traditional American notions of summer be discarded, these efforts can help to ensure a far better match of our nostalgic—and wonderful—summer visions and our children's reality.

### Notes

1. Cooper, H., Nye, B., Charlton, K., Lindsay, J., & Greathouse, S. (1996). The effects of summer vacation on achievement test scores: A narrative and meta-analytic review. *Review of Educational Research, 66,* 227–268.

2. Entwisle, D., & Alexander, K. (1992). Summer setback: Race, poverty, school composition, and mathematics achievement in the first two years of school. *American Sociological Review, 57,* 72–84.

3. Food Research and Action Center. (2005). *Hunger doesn't take a vacation: Summer nutrition status report.* Retrieved May 8, 2007, from http://www.frac.org/pdf/summerfood06.pdf.

4. Harrington-Leuker, D. (2000). Summer learners. *American School Board Journal, 183*(3), 20–25.

5. Borman, G. (2001). Summers are for learning. *Principal Magazine, 80*(3), 26–29.

6. Cooper, H., Charlton, K., Valentine, J. C., & Muhlenbruck, L. (2000). Making the most of summer school: A meta-analytic and narrative review. *Monographs of the Society for Research in Child Development, 65*(1, Serial No. 260).

7. Gold, K. (2002). *School's in: The history of summer education in American public schools.* New York: Lang.
8. American Camp Association. *Camp trends fact sheet.* Retrieved May 8, 2007, from http://www.acacamps.org/media_center/camp_trends.
9. For 2005, BCPSS made summer school available to virtually all Title I elementary school children, to all children in transitional grades (from elementary to middle and middle to high school), and, for a modest fee, to all high school students who needed credit recovery classes to make up a failed grade.

M. JANE SUNDIUS *provides funding and technical assistance to Baltimore's out-of-school-time programs as director of education and youth development at the Open Society Institute-Baltimore.*

# Index

# New Directions for Youth Development
## Order Form
### SUBSCRIPTIONS AND SINGLE ISSUES

**DISCOUNTED BACK ISSUES:**

*Use this form to receive **20% off** all back issues of New Directions for Youth Development. All single issues priced at **$23.20** (normally $29.00)*

TITLE                                          ISSUE NO.      ISBN

_____   _____   _____

_____   _____   _____

_____   _____   _____

***Call 888-378-2537*** *or see mailing instructions below. When calling, mention the promotional code, JB7ND, to receive your discount.*

*For a complete list of issues, please visit **www.josseybass.com/go/ndyd***

**SUBSCRIPTIONS:** *(1 year, 4 issues)*

☐ New Order      ☐ Renewal

|                  |                         |                            |
|------------------|-------------------------|----------------------------|
| U.S.             | ☐ Individual: $80       | ☐ Institutional: $195      |
| Canada/Mexico    | ☐ Individual: $80       | ☐ Institutional: $235      |
| All Others       | ☐ Individual: $104      | ☐ Institutional: $269      |

***Call 888-378-2537*** *or see mailing and pricing instructions below. Online subscriptions are available at www.interscience.wiley.com.*

Copy or detach page and send to:
**John Wiley & Sons, Journals Dept, 5th Floor**
**989 Market Street, San Francisco, CA 94103-1741**

Order Form can also be faxed to: 888-481-2665

| Issue/Subscription Amount: $ _____ | **SHIPPING CHARGES:** | | |
|---|---|---|---|
| Shipping Amount: $ _____ | SURFACE | Domestic | Canadian |
| (for single issues only—subscription prices include shipping) | First Item | $5.00 | $6.00 |
| **Total Amount:** $ _____ | Each Add'l Item | $3.00 | $1.50 |

(No sales tax for U.S. subscriptions. Canadian residents, add GST for subscription orders. Individual rate subscriptions must be paid by personal check or credit card. Individual rate subscriptions may not be resold as library copies.)

☐ Payment enclosed (U.S. check or money order only. All payments must be in U.S. dollars.)

☐ VISA  ☐ MC  ☐ Amex # _____ Exp. Date_____

Card Holder Name _____ Card Issue # _____

Signature_____ Day Phone _____

☐ Bill Me (U.S. institutional orders only. Purchase order required.)

Purchase order # _____
Federal Tax ID13559302      GST 89102 8052

Name_____

Address _____

Phone _____ E-mail _____

# NEW DIRECTIONS FOR YOUTH DEVELOPMENT
# IS NOW AVAILABLE ONLINE AT WILEY INTERSCIENCE

## What is Wiley InterScience?

*Wiley InterScience* is the dynamic online content service from John Wiley & Sons delivering the full text of over 300 leading scientific, technical, medical, and professional journals, plus major reference works, the acclaimed *Current Protocols* laboratory manuals, and even the full text of select Wiley print books online.

## What are some special features of Wiley InterScience?

*Wiley InterScience Alerts* is a service that delivers table of contents via e-mail for any journal available on Wiley InterScience as soon as a new issue is published online.

*Early View* is Wiley's exclusive service presenting individual articles online as soon as they are ready, even before the release of the compiled print issue. These articles are complete, peer-reviewed, and citable.

*CrossRef* is the innovative multi-publisher reference linking system enabling readers to move seamlessly from a reference in a journal article to the cited publication, typically located on a different server and published by a different publisher.

## How can I access Wiley InterScience?

Visit http://www.interscience.wiley.com

*Guest Users* can browse Wiley InterScience for unrestricted access to journal Tables of Contents and Article Abstracts, or use the powerful search engine.

*Registered Users* are provided with a *Personal Home Page* to store and manage customized alerts, searches, and links to favorite journals and articles. Additionally, Registered Users can view free Online Sample Issues and preview selected material from major reference works.

*Licensed Customers* are entitled to access full-text journal articles in PDF, with select journals also offering full-text HTML.

## How do I become an Authorized User?

*Authorized Users* are individuals authorized by a paying Customer to have access to the journals in Wiley InterScience. For example, a university that subscribes to Wiley journals is considered to be the Customer. Faculty, staff, and students authorized by the university to have access to those journals in Wiley InterScience are Authorized Users. Users should contact their Library for information on which Wiley journals they have access to in Wiley InterScience.

**ASK YOUR INSTITUTION ABOUT WILEY INTERSCIENCE TODAY!**